THE TV MAITRE D'
COOKBOOK

Joe Zito
Host/Executive Producer of The TV Maitre d' Television Show

THE TV MAITRE D'
COOKBOOK

Your Guide to the Best Restaurants and Chefs in Southern New England
Featuring Their Secret Recipes

BY JOE ZITO AND LINDA BEAULIEU

Joe Zito and Linda Beaulieu
The TV Maitre d' Cookbook
1615 South Road
East Greenwich, RI 02818
(401) 595-3399

GRAPHIC DESIGNER
Impress Graphics, Inc.

PHOTOGRAPHY
Brian Beaulieu
Linda Beaulieu
Armand DeLuise
Ron Manville/Providence Monthly
Joe Zito

RECIPE TESTING
Linda Beaulieu
Cheryl Ryan
John Ryan
Cynthia Salvato
Nancy Sandbach
Joe and Nancy Zito

OFFICE ASSISTANT
Mark Zito

Printed in the United States of America
First edition

DEDICATION

For Nancy, who is simply the best,
and Mark, who is already thinking
about how to turn this into a movie.

For all our friends and relatives,
who so willingly helped us test
and taste these wonderful recipes.

For Brian and Beau,
who ate lots of leftovers.

Some of the key ingredients...

Joe and his Dad,
who refers to himself as "the real Joe Zito"

Mark and Nancy

Angelo

Mom

There's an old saying that "too many chefs spoil the soup."
But it's another story when talking about this book.

With more than 100 talented chefs and wonderful restaurants represented, I firmly believe that **The TV Maitre d' Cookbook** is more than a hundred times better because of it.

For years on my television show, my tagline has been "always the very best table in your house!" Now, it will be amended to "always the very best recipes in your kitchen!"

And that's what this book is all about. This is a cookbook! So, if you plan on sticking it on the coffee table and not using it, you'll be missing out.

The recipes herein have all been personally tested, a creative and electric culinary blend representing every food and mood. In addition, my good friend, Mark Gasbarro, whose Federal Hill wine shop in Providence is among the finest in the country, will recommend wines for many of the featured appetizers and entrees. Without exception, good food needs good wine. Now, we're covered. Cent'anni!

For me, cooking has always been a form of therapy. I love to cook, I'm just not sure you'd love to eat what I cook! See, every one of my recipes includes a big glass of red wine and a generous dose of Dean Martin blaring in the kitchen.

Yeah, spatula in one hand, Chianti in the other... "Now, that's amore." I urge you to try it.

The other thing that cooking has always done for me is create special memories. My hope is that every recipe in this book will supply memories for your family and friends. Full of laughter, good times, and good food.

That's what it's all about. Which brings me to the part where I thank some very special people whose belief in me in the way distant past and right now have made this project a reality. And they are:

Mom... Gloria left us in 1994. But, what burns eternal for me was her unwavering devotion to her family and her incredible ability to whip up unbelievable Italian food from scratch. At a moment's notice! Growing up, her kitchen was the heart and soul of our home. Everyone was welcome and no one ever left hungry. No, Mom would have never used her son's cookbook... but she probably would have had it bronzed. Ah, sweet, sweet Gloria!

Dad... The guy, who's been my hero and role model since I was two, has already demanded a free copy. Cheapskate! Signed, no less! Imagine! Do you think it might be some sort of poetic justice to tell this man who's run the desk at Twin Oaks, one of the country's busiest restaurants, for more than 40 years to show up at my booksigning and wait his turn? "Zito, pawty of one... Zito, pawty of one."

Angelo... He was my grandfather, and he made the best Aglio Olio I have ever had. Yes, with anchovies! I can still sense the aroma wafting through the kitchen. I was eight. Keep in mind that this was the pre-Altoid era. I never knew why no girls talked to me until I was fourteen. Miss you, Pop!

Ah, fond memories. As for the present, a few more important thank you's...

To **all** of the **terrific restaurants and chefs** who've taken time to supply recipes... thank you. No one was told what to submit, and what came back was far beyond expectations.

To my friend, **Armand DeLuise**, the talented camera operator and editor who puts up with my crazy whims to put out a great TV show month in and month out... thanks for being a key ingredient in the master recipe.

To **Alan Costantino**, owner of Venda Ravioli and my friend, whose belief in me and my work has made so much possible. I am truly grateful.

And lastly, very special thanks to my co-author, **Linda Beaulieu**, a good friend and a wonderful writer without whom I really wouldn't have this fabulous cookbook. Instead, I'd have a 152-page TV Maitre d' scratch pad. From day one, she was heaven sent!

Yes, I'm proud of this book for so many reasons and so many recipes.

Enjoy!

Joe Zito
The TV Maitre d'
October 2007

Sharing a laugh with...

Bob Burke, Pot au Feu

Tony Papa, Tony Papa's Restaurant

Michael and Patrick Berek,
Remington House Inn

TABLE OF CONTENTS

Breaking bread with...

Alan Costantino,
owner of Venda Ravioli and Costantino's Ristorante

Two of the luckiest people on earth happen to be the authors of this cookbook, Joe Zito and Linda Beaulieu. I've known both for years, and they have both done much to help promote the hospitality industry in southern New England. It is just wonderful that these two talented individuals decided to collaborate on this project.

Venda has been on every episode of Joe's popular television show, **The TV Maitre d'**, since it began in February 2004. Through that highly rated show, Joe exposes everyone in his viewing area — all of southern New England — to our unparalleled restaurant scene. First through his TV show and now via this combination restaurant guide/cookbook, Joe introduces people who love a good meal to many restaurants they may not have even heard about. It isn't often that an individual comes along who has both the experience and enthusiasm to explain to others what's happening on the constantly changing food scene. Joe is that individual. He continually strives to make the next episode of **The TV Maitre d'** better than the last. And he does justice to all styles of cooking and types of cuisine, although we can't help but notice his love for all things Italian.

While Joe takes care of Venda's audio/video needs, Linda is the person we go to when words need to be written. Whether it's a newsletter or our web site, www.vendaravioli.com, Linda writes intelligently and passionately about what's new in the world of food. It might be a new brand of cheese imported from Italy, or an upcoming appearance by a famous Italian author. Whatever the topic, Linda is always there to help us get the word out.

In the spring of 2007, Joe and Linda told me of their plans to write **The TV Maitre d'** Cookbook. I was honored when they asked me to write the foreword to their book which is filled with a terrific assortment of recipes from the very best restaurants in this area.

Both Joe and Linda were brought up at the family table, and that is very important to me. That's just one reason why I like these two hard-working individuals as much as I do. Joe and Linda both love food, and they love their "jobs." Fortunately for them, it happens to be one and the same thing. And that is evident in the quality of their work, whether it's a TV show, a magazine article, or this cookbook. I wish them much success, and I hope they will always be here to enlighten us.

Alan Costantino
October 2007

FROM
THE COVER...

Sai Viswanath,
DeWolf Tavern

Gian Carlo Iannuccilli,
Gian Carlo's

Nick Iannuccilli,
Rodizio

Ralph Conte,
Raphael Bar Risto

John Elkhay,
Chow Fun Food Group

Jules Ramos,
Eleven Forty Nine

Phyllis Arffa,
Blaze

Brian Kingsford,
Bacaro

Jeff Burgess,
Zooma

Alberto Lopez,
Venda Ravioli

Louis Forti,
Venda Ravioli

Salvatore Cefaliello,
Venda Ravioli

Bob Burke,
Pot au Feu

Life is short, so eat dessert first. This wonderful new take on the classic crème brulee comes from Craig McLaren, executive sous chef at Agora.

PEACH AND TAHITIAN VANILLA CRÈME BRULEE

(12 servings)

2 cups heavy cream
1 cup whole milk
1 vanilla bean, split (Tahitian vanilla bean is recommended)
5 fresh peaches
½ cup granulated sugar, divided
10 ounces (1 and ¼ cups) egg yolks
1 large egg
Granulated sugar, for topping
Fresh mint, optional garnish

Preheat oven to 300 degrees.

In a large saucepan, combine the cream, milk and vanilla bean over medium-high heat. Bring to a simmer. Remove from heat and cool, allowing the vanilla flavor to become more pronounced. Peel and seed the peaches. Using ¼ cup of the sugar, puree the peaches in a food processor. Set aside.

In a large bowl, whisk together the eggs and remaining sugar. Add the peach puree and slowly add the cream mixture, whisking constantly, to make a custard. Strain the custard and pour equally into 12 ramekins. Place the ramekins into a water bath (a large pan filled with at least 1 inch of water), and cover the pan loosely with aluminum foil. Place the pan on the center rack of the 300-degree oven. Bake for 45 to 50 minutes, or until the sides are firm and the centers are still loose. Remove the foil and allow the ramekins to cool in the water bath. Wrap individually and chill for at least 2 hours.

To serve, dust the surface of each custard with granulated sugar and melt the sugar using a kitchen blowtorch. If a blowtorch is not available, place the ramekins under a hot broiler until the sugar melts and forms a golden crust. Garnish with fresh mint, if desired.

AGORA

The Westin Providence
1 West Exchange Street
Providence, RI
401-598-8011
On the web:
starwoodhotels.com/westin

Owner: The Procaccianti Group

Cuisine: Contemporary American

Specialty: Utilizing local
                  seafood and fresh
                  Rhode Island produce

Signature dish: Pan-Roasted
                  Wild Striped Bass
                  with Wilted Mushrooms

Price range: Appetizers,
                     $3 to $18

                        Entrees,
                     $24 to $38

Hours: Open seven days
               a week for breakfast,
               lunch and dinner,
               from 6:30 am to 10 pm

AL FORNO

577 South Main Street
Providence, RI
401-273-9760
www.alforno.com

Chef/Owners: Johanne Killeen
and George Germon

Cuisine: Northern Italian

Specialty: Wood-fired dishes

Signature dish: Grilled Pizza

Price range: Appetizers,
$7 to $23

Entrees,
$20 to $33

Hours: Tuesday through Friday,
5 to 10 pm

Saturday,
4 to 10 pm

This recipe is used with the gracious permission of George and Johanne, the chef-owners of Al Forno. It's from their wonderful cookbook, "On Top of Spaghetti."

BAKED PASTA BIANCA WITH CREAM AND FIVE CHEESES
(4 to 6 servings)

2 and ½ cups heavy cream
½ to 1 cup homemade chicken stock
¼ cup finely crumbled Gorgonzola
½ cup freshly grated Parmigiano-Reggiano
½ cup freshly grated Pecorino Romano
2 tablespoons mascarpone
½ cup chopped mozzarella
½ teaspoon sea salt, or more to taste
1 pound dried pasta shells or penne rigate

Preheat oven to 500 degrees. Bring a large pot of water to a boil.

In a large mixing bowl, combine the cream, ½ cup chicken stock, all the cheeses, and salt. Mix well. Taste and add more salt if necessary. Set aside.

Generously salt the boiling water, and drop in the pasta. Cook, stirring often, for 4 to 5 minutes. The pasta will be parboiled and too hard to eat; it cooks further in the oven. Drain the pasta, and transfer the pasta to the mixing bowl. Combine thoroughly with the sauce mixture. If it seems too thick, add some more chicken stock, a tablespoon at a time, until the pasta moves freely and is surrounded by liquid.

Transfer to individual shallow baking dishes or 1 or 2 large shallow baking dishes. Bake for 8 to 10 minutes, or until the pasta is bubbly hot. Serve immediately.

Recommended wine: *Allegrini Palazzo della Torre*

The Yukons and the asparagus are like a symphony in concert with the scallops. Wow!

SEARED SEA SCALLOPS WITH GRILLED ASPARAGUS

(I serving)

4 dry-packed sea scallops (U-10 are recommended)
Sea salt and freshly cracked black pepper, to taste
Olive oil, as needed
6 asparagus stalks, with ends trimmed
Sweet red wine vinaigrette, as needed
I cup peeled and chopped Yukon Gold potatoes
Butter and cream, to taste
Chervil goat cheese, crumbled, as needed
Chopped chives, as needed
I shallot, cut into thin slices
3 cups Chardonnay wine
I pound unsalted butter
I lemon
Truffle butter (available in gourmet shops), to taste
Minced rosemary, as needed

Season the scallops with sea salt and pepper. Cook the scallops until they are caramelized in a very hot cast-iron frying pan that has been seasoned with olive oil. Set aside; keep warm.

Marinate the asparagus in the red wine vinaigrette. Cook carefully over a grill until done to your taste. Set aside; keep warm.

In a pot of boiling water, cook the potatoes until soft. Run the cooked potatoes through a ricer until smoothly mashed. Add butter, cream, salt and pepper, to taste. Fold in the goat cheese and chives. Set aside; keep warm.

In a frying pan, sauté the shallots in a little olive oil. Deglaze the pan with the wine. Allow the wine to reduce. Add the unsalted butter and the juice of a lemon, using a whisk to fully incorporate. Add the truffle butter, minced rosemary, salt and pepper to taste.

On a warm dinner plate, serve the seared sea scallops with the grilled asparagus and whipped potatoes.

Chef's note: At Amalfi, this dish is garnished with drops of chive-infused oil, a crisp lattice potato, and a fresh rosemary sprig.

Recommended wine: *Tenuta Perolla Bianco Toscana*

AUNT CARRIE'S

1240 Ocean Road
Narragansett, RI
401-783-7930
www.auntcarriesri.com

Chef: No chef,
            just lots of great cooks

Owner: Elsie Foy

Cuisine: Seafood

Specialty: Local fresh seafood

Signature dish: Clam Cakes

Price range: Appetizers,
                       $2 to $10

Entrees, $6.50 to market
price for clams and lobster

Hours: Open April through
September (call for hours).

From Memorial Day
to Labor Day,
open six days a week,
noon to 9 pm.

Closed on Tuesday.

*This creation is just like the restaurant it comes from...
nothing fancy but incredibly delicious.*

INDIAN PUDDING
(8 to 10 servings)

3 and ½ cups milk
¾ cup corn meal
3 and 1/2 cups hot water
3 tablespoons butter
3 eggs
1 and ¼ cups dark molasses
1 teaspoon salt
¾ teaspoon cinnamon
½ teaspoon ground ginger
Vanilla ice cream, as needed

Preheat oven to 350 degrees.

In a large bowl, mix the milk and corn meal with a whisk. Whisk this mixture into the hot water in the top of a large double boiler set over simmering water. Whisk every few minutes until the mixture thickens, about 15 to 20 minutes. Remove from the heat. Add the butter.

In a large bowl, lightly beat the eggs. Whisk in the molasses, salt, cinnamon and ginger. The mixture should be grainy and loose, not too thick. If too thick, add another cup of milk. Pour the mixture into an 11-by-7-inch baking dish. Bake in the 350-degree oven until a skin forms on the top, about 1 hour. Cool. Serve with ice cream.

Trust me, the Lobster from Hell is, in a word, heavenly.

BACARO

262 South Water Street
Providence, RI
401-751-3700
www.bacarorestaurant.net

ARAGOSTA DA INFERNO
(LOBSTER FROM HELL)

(I serving)

I lobster, I to I and ½ pounds, per person

For every lobster, you will need:

3 tablespoons extra virgin olive oil

½ cup whole peeled tomatoes in heavy
    puree, crushed

I pinch red pepper flakes

½ teaspoon minced garlic

¼ cup white wine
    (Pinot Grigio is recommended)

3 tablespoons unsalted butter

¼ cup chopped fresh parsley

For the garnish:

Chopped fresh parsley

Extra virgin olive oil

Prepare a hot charcoal fire. (A grill rack will not be necessary.) When the coals are red-hot (you will be able to hold your hand 3 to 5 inches over the fire for a count of three), rake the coals out evenly across the bottom of the grill. It is important to have only enough coal to form one layer across the bottom of the grill. The more coal that is stacked on top of each other, the hotter the fire will be, changing the cooking times in this recipe.

Split the lobster in half lengthwise, and remove the rubber bands on the claws. Remove the 2 arms and claws. Crack the claws with the back of a heavy chef's knife or use lobster crackers.

You will need an extra heavy-duty foil bag, 15 by 17 inches in size, for each lobster you prepare. Lay out the ingredients, multiplying the amounts needed for the number of lobsters you plan to cook. It is best to have the ingredients measured out separately for each bag to make sure the right amount is going in with each lobster. Gently place the 2 lobster halves into each bag, along with the ingredients. Reserve a pinch of parsley for garnish at the end of the cooking process. Be careful not to puncture the bag. If the bag is punctured, discard that bag and start the process over with a new bag. Crimp the bag closed by pulling together the 2 sides and rolling them over one another. Place the bag directly onto the coals of the fire, again being careful not to puncture the bag.

Cook for 8 to 9 minutes, then remove the bag from the hot coals, but do not open. Allow the bag to sit for 3 minutes before opening. After 3 minutes, open the bag and place the 2 lobster halves on a large dinner plate. Pour the sauce from the bag over the top. Garnish with the reserved parsley and a drizzle of extra virgin olive oil.

Chef/Owner:	Brian Kingsford
Cuisine:	Italian
Specialty:	Wood-fired cooking
Signature dish:	Salumeria and Cichetti (Italian tapas)
Price range:	Appetizers, $12 to $20
	Entrees, $19 to $35
Hours:	Tuesday through Saturday, 4 to 10 pm

Recommended wine: *Vietti Roero Arneis*

BASIL'S

22 Kingstown Road
Narragansett, RI
401-789-3743

Chef: Vasilios Kourakis

Owners: Vasilios and
        Kathleen Kourakis

Cuisine: French Continental

Specialty: Classic French dishes

Signature dish: Veal Basil's

Price range: Appetizers,
        $6 to $11

        Entrees,
        $18 to $39

Hours: Seasonal hours
        (call to check)

        Winter:
Wednesday through Sunday,
        5:30 to 10 pm

        Summer:
Tuesday through Sunday,
        5:30 to 10 pm

Their take on this classical French masterpiece will make you scream, "Ooo la la!"

DUCK A L'ORANGE
(ROASTED DUCK WITH ORANGE SAUCE)

(4 servings)

1 duck, 5 to 6 pounds	¼ cup white wine vinegar
Salt and pepper, to taste	¼ cup fresh lemon juice
2 cups brown sauce	2 teaspoons orange marmalade
2 oranges	3 tablespoons unsalted butter
¼ cup sugar	1 tablespoon Grand Mariner

Preheat oven to 450 degrees.

With a sharp knife, cut off each wing tip on the duck at the joint. Rub the cavities of the duck with salt and pepper, and sprinkle the skin of the duck lightly with salt. Place the duck breast side up on a rack set in a large shallow roasting pan. Roast in the middle of the 450-degree oven for 35 minutes until the skin browns lightly. Drain off the fat from the pan, and turn the duck over. Reduce the heat to 350 degrees, and roast for another 35 minutes. Turn the duck breast side up again, and continue roasting for another 35 minutes, removing the fat as it accumulates in the pan. To test for doneness, pierce the thigh with the point of a knife. The juice that trickles out should be a clear yellow. If it is pink, roast the duck for another 10 minutes. Transfer the duck to a heated platter, and cover with foil while you make the orange sauce.

Tilt the pan and, with a large spoon, remove and discard all the fat from the juices that remain. Pour in the brown sauce,e and bring to simmer over moderate heat, while scraping the browned particles clinging to the bottom and sides of the pan. Set the pan aside, off the heat.

With a small knife, remove the peel from one of the oranges in long strips as wide as possible without cutting into the bitter white section. Cut the peel into very thin strips about 2 inches long. You should have ¼ cup of orange peel strips. Drop the peels into boiling water and cook for 1 to 2 minutes, then drain the peels and run cold water over the strips to set their color. Spread the strips on paper towels to dry. Squeeze enough juice from the oranges to make ⅓ cup and set aside.

In a 3-quart saucepan, combine the sugar and vinegar. Bring to a boil over high heat. Cook until the mixture thickens to a golden syrup. Pour the warm brown sauce into the pan. Reduce the heat to low, and simmer 3 to 4 minutes, stirring constantly. Stir in the reserved orange juice, lemon juice and orange marmalade. Strain this sauce through a fine sieve into another saucepan. Swirl in the butter and, when completely absorbed, the Grand Mariner. Season to taste with salt and pepper. If desired, pour some of the sauce around the roasted duck and serve the remainder in a sauceboat. Scatter the orange peel over the duck, and serve immediately.

Recommended wine: *Steele Bienacido Pinot Noir*

Just saying the name of this recipe will make your mouth water. Enjoy!

BAY LEAVES

8220 Post Road
North Kingstown, RI
401-667-7225
www.bayleavesrestaurant.com

FIG AND APRICOT STUFFED CHICKEN WITH LEMON THYME SAUCE

(4 servings)

½ cup oil

1 onion, cut into thin julienne strips

½ cup dried figs, sliced

½ cup dried apricots, sliced

½ cup dried currants

¼ cup slivered almonds

1 tablespoon cinnamon

1 tablespoon cumin

2 tablespoons sugar

¾ cup water

Kosher salt, to taste

4 whole chicken breasts, boneless, skin on

1 cup water

Sauce:

½ cup white wine

¼ cup lemon juice

3 thyme sprigs

1 cup cream

Kosher salt, to taste

In a large frying pan, heat the oil and sauté the onions until soft. Add the dried fruits and almonds. Stir to blend with the oil. Add the spices and sugar. Sauté lightly until spices become aromatic. Add the water and salt. Cook slowly until the water is completely reduced. Spread the dried fruit mixture on a baking sheet, and cool completely.

Preheat oven to 375 degrees.

Place the chicken skin side down between 2 layers of plastic wrap. Pound gently until evenly flattened. Place about ½ cup of stuffing in the center of each chicken breast. Wrap the chicken around the stuffing. Put the chicken folded side down into a baking pan. Cover the chicken with aluminum foil that has been rubbed with a bit of oil to keep the skin from sticking. Add about 1 cup of water to the baking pan to help the chicken remain moist. Bake in the 375-degree oven for 20 to 25 minutes. Remove the foil, and place under the broiler for 15 to 20 seconds to brown the skin. If you don't have a broiler, turn the oven to the highest temperature to brown the skin.

In a small saucepan over medium-high heat, combine the wine, lemon juice and thyme. Reduce by half. Add the cream, and cook slowly until the sauce thickens. Add salt to taste. Remove thyme sprigs before serving the sauce with the chicken.

Recommended wine: *Molly Dooker the Boxer Shiraz*

Chef: Tammie Watson

Owners: Kamer and
          Veysel Kosereisoglu

Cuisine: Eastern Mediterranean

Specialty: Lamb dishes and mezzes

Price range: Appetizers,
          $6 to $10

          Entrees,
          $14 to $25

Hours: Tuesday through Thursday,
          11:30 am to 9:30 pm

          Friday and Saturday,
          11:30 am to 10:30 pm

          Sunday,
          4 to 9:30 pm

BERTUCCI'S

1946 Post Road
Warwick, RI
401-732-4343
www.bertuccis.com

Chef: Vice President and
Corporate Chef
Stefano Cordova

Owner: Bertucci's Corporation

Cuisine: Italian

Specialty: New grilled Italian
favorites and classic
Italian dishes

Signature dish: Brick Oven Pizza

Price range: Appetizers,
$6 to $10

Entrees,
$11 to $20

Hours: Open seven days a week

Monday through Thursday,
11 am to 10 pm

Friday and Saturday,
11 am to 11 pm

Sunday,
noon to 10 pm

*This is a personal favorite of mine,
and they were kind enough to let me publish the recipe.*

ROSEMARY CHICKEN PANINI AL FORNO
(1 serving)

1 (6-ounce) chicken breast
1 teaspoon extra virgin olive oil
1 teaspoon chopped rosemary
6 round zucchini slices, ⅛-inch thick
1 pita bread
4 slices plum tomato
½ teaspoon fresh chopped garlic
½ teaspoon fresh sliced basil
Pinch of crushed red pepper flakes
Pinch of sea salt
2 slices provolone cheese
1 tablespoon pesto sauce

Season the chicken with the oil and rosemary. Cook the chicken on a preheated grill for 2 to 3 minutes on each side, or until the breast is firm but not dry. Let the chicken cool slightly, then slice it into long thin strips. Grill the zucchini slices on both sides until lightly brown. Set aside.

Cut off the tip of the pita bread to form an open pocket. Season the chicken, zucchini and tomatoes with the garlic, basil, crushed red pepper flakes and sea salt. Inside the pita, layer a slice of provolone, sliced chicken, zucchini and tomatoes. Finish the layers with the second slice of provolone.

Reduce the heat of the grill to 250 degrees. Place the sandwich over the grill and cook it on both sides until the cheese has melted. Cut the sandwich in half, and place on a plate. Spoon the pesto around the sandwich, and serve immediately.

Recommended wine: *La Battistina Gavi*

Hearty, flavorful, fresh and delicious... another big dish from Big Fish!

SEAFOOD BOLOGNESE
(4 servings)

16 littleneck clams
Salt, as needed
1 and ½ pounds fettuccine
Olive oil, as needed
8 large scallops (10 to 20 per pound)
16 extra large shrimp (21 to 25 per pound), peeled and deveined
Salt and pepper, to taste
1 cup lobster meat
1 and ½ cups Bolognese sauce (see note below)
4 tablespoons butter
2 tablespoons chopped parsley

In a medium-size pot filled with about 1 inch of water, cook the clams over medium-high heat until they open. Remove the clams from the water, and set them aside.

In another large pot, bring 1 and ½ gallons of water and 2 tablespoons of salt to a boil. Add the fettuccine and cook until al dente, about 7 minutes. Strain the pasta in a colander. Place the pasta in a large heated bowl, and mix with a little olive oil.

While the fettuccine is cooking, season the scallops and shrimp with salt and pepper. In a large sauté pan over medium high heat, sear the scallops until golden brown on both sides. Add the shrimp and lobster meat. Sauté briefly. Add the Bolognese sauce to the pan, and continue to cook until the shrimp turn pink and are fully cooked. Add the butter to the sauce, stirring constantly until incorporated into the sauce. Separate the pasta into 4 large warm serving bowls. Pour equal amounts of sauce and seafood into each bowl. Garnish with the littleneck clams and parsley. Serve immediately.

Note: This is not your classic Bolognese sauce. To make Big Fish Bolognese: In a large pot, sauté ¼ cup chopped garlic in olive oil until golden brown. Deglaze the pan with 1 and ½ cups white wine, and reduce by half. Add 3 cups heavy cream, bring to a boil, and reduce heat to a simmer. Reduce until the sauce is thick. Add 1 tablespoon lobster base (available in gourmet shops).

Recommended wine: *Terruzi and Puthod Terre di Tufi*

BIG

370 Richmond
Providence, RI
401-751-3474
www.bigfishri.com

Chef: David Jackson

Owners: John Elkhay,
                 Rick and Cheryl Bready

Cuisine: Contemporary
                 American

Specialty: Pasta, pizza
                 and seafood

Signature dish: Everything Tuna
                 over Creamed Spinach

Price range: Appetizers,
                 $5.50 to $12

                 Entrees,
                 $16 to $26

Hours: Lunch on
                 Monday through Friday,
                 11:30 am to 4 pm

                 Dinner on
                 Monday through Thursday,
                 4 to 10 pm;
                 Friday and Saturday,
                 4 to 11 pm

I know... you think it's named after me.
This is a good-time recipe for a crowd at your next party.

KNUCKLEHEAD CHILI
(6 to 8 servings)

1 pound ground beef
1 pound flap meat
(similar to skirt or flank steak)

1 teaspoon cumin
1 teaspoon chili powder
2 teaspoons Cajun seasoning
1 teaspoon garlic powder
2 tablespoons honey
¼ cup barbecue sauce

2 large peppers, diced
1 large onion, diced

2 teaspoons cumin
2 teaspoons crushed red pepper
1 tablespoon garlic powder
1 tablespoon black pepper
2 teaspoons paprika
1 tablespoon Cajun seasoning
1 tablespoon cayenne pepper
2 tablespoons chili powder
2 tablespoons beef base
1 (6-ounce) can tomato paste
¼ cup honey
½ cup barbecue sauce

1 (28-ounce) can crushed tomatoes
1 (28-ounce) can ground tomatoes
1 (28-ounce) can red kidney beans, rinsed

In a very large frying pan, or in batches, cook the ground beef until brown in color (155 degrees on a meat thermometer). Set aside.

In a very large frying pan, or in batches, cook the flap meat with the next six ingredients (155 degrees on a meat thermometer). Dice the flap meat after it is cooked.

In a very large stockpot, combine the diced peppers, onions, remaining spices, beef base, tomato paste, honey and barbecue sauce. Simmer for 30 minutes, then add the crushed and ground tomatoes. Simmer another 30 minutes, then add the ground beef and flap meat mixture. Simmer for 1 hour. Remove the stockpot from the heat. Add the kidney beans to the mixture, stirring gently. Serve in heated bowls.

Chef's note: All the spices in this recipe can be adjusted more or less to taste.

Recommended beer: Sierra Nevada Pale Ale

Chef: Bob Altomari

Owner: Milia Daoud

Cuisine: Standard American fare

Specialty: Burgers and steaks

Signature dish: Steak a la Mama

Price range: Appetizers,
                    $2 to $11

                    Entrees,
                    $7 to $17

Hours: Open seven days a week

Monday through Thursday,
    11 am to 1 am

Friday and Saturday,
    11 am to 2 am

Sunday,
noon to 1 am

One bite will transport you to the French Quarter in New Orleans.

CRISP CATFISH AND ANDOUILLE SAUSAGE JAMBALAYA

(4 servings)

1 onion, diced
2 celery stalks, diced
1 tablespoon minced garlic
Oil, as needed
1 link andouille sausage, cut into ¼-inch slices
1 tablespoon tomato paste
4 tablespoons (½ stick) butter
½ teaspoon chopped fresh thyme
1 teaspoon gumbo file*
Pinch of cayenne, or more to taste
2 cups water
1 cup par-boiled rice
4 catfish filets
Corn meal, as needed
Salt and pepper, to taste

In a large stockpot, sauté the onion, celery and garlic in a little bit of oil until soft. Add the sausage. Add the tomato paste, butter and spices. Mix well. Add the water and rice. Bring to a boil; reduce heat to a simmer. Cook until the water has evaporated.

While the jambalaya is cooking, dredge the catfish in the corn meal. In a large frying pan or deep-fryer, fry the catfish in oil until crispy on both sides. Drain the catfish on paper towels. Sprinkle with salt and pepper while hot. Keep warm until ready to serve with the jambalaya.

*Gumbo file is an essential Cajun spice made from dried sassafras leaves. It's available in the spice department of supermarkets and gourmet shops.

Recommended wine: *Casa del Hermita Crianza*

BLAZE

776 Hope Street
401-277-2529

272 Thayer Street
401-490-2128
Providence, RI
www.blazerestaurants.com

Chef: Phyllis Arffa

Owners: Christine Edmonds
               and Phyllis Arffa

Cuisine: American fusion

Specialty: Southern American,
               Caribbean influenced dishes

Price range: Appetizers,
                        $5 to $10

                        Entrees,
                        $8 to $24

Hours: On Hope Street
Tuesday through Thursday,
11 am to 9 pm

Friday, 11 am to 10 pm

Saturday, 5 to 10 pm,
and Sunday, 5 to 9 pm

On Thayer Street
Monday through Thursday,
11 am to 10 pm

Friday, 11 am to 11 pm

Saturday, noon to 11 pm,
and Sunday, noon to 9 pm

BLUEFIN GRILLE

One Orms Street
Providence, RI
401-272-5852
www.marriottprovidence.com

Chefs: Executive Chef
                Franco Paterno

                Executive Sous Chef
                James Cook

                Chef de Cuisine
                Rebecca Lentrichia

Owner: Meyer Jabara

Cuisine: Contemporary
                American

Specialty: Seafood

Signature dish: Bluefin Calamari

Price range: Appetizers,
                $8 to $12

                Entrees,
                $19 to $30

Hours: Open seven days a week

        Breakfast, 6:30 to 11:30 am

        Lunch, 11:30 am to 2 pm

        Dinner, 5 to 10 pm

This Rhode Island striper never had it so good! The relish is the perfect complement.

RHODE ISLAND STRIPED BASS WITH TOMATO CAPER RELISH

(4 servings)

Tomato caper relish:
- 1 cup chopped ripe tomatoes
- 1 tablespoon finely diced sun-dried tomatoes
- 1 tablespoon finely minced shallots
- 1 tablespoon drained capers
- 2 tablespoons rice vinegar
- 1 tablespoon fresh lemon juice
- 1 tablespoon finely minced fresh basil
- 1 tablespoon finely minced fresh chives
- 2 tablespoons extra virgin olive oil

Kosher salt and black pepper, as needed
1 pound fingerling potatoes
Unsalted butter, as needed
½ pound haricot vert (French beans or local string beans when in season)
2 pounds striped bass, cut into 4 equal portions (8 ounces each)
1 tablespoon extra virgin olive oil

In a mixing bowl, combine all the ingredients for the tomato caper relish. Season to taste with salt and pepper. Set aside. Preheat oven to 300 degrees.

In a pot of boiling water, cook the potatoes until done, approximately 15 minutes. Drain the potatoes. Dress the hot potatoes with unsalted butter. Season to taste with salt and pepper. Keep warm.

In a pot of boiling salted water, blanch the beans for 2 minutes. Drain the beans, and immediately "shock" them in an ice bath. Gently reheat the beans in a sauté pan with a little unsalted butter.

In a nonstick ovenproof skillet, sear the fish in 1 tablespoon extra virgin olive oil. Turn the fish over, and finish cooking in the 300-degree oven for approximately 8 minutes. Place the warm potatoes on each dinner plate. Top with the beans, then the striped bass. Top with a generous amount of the relish. Serve immediately.

Recommended wine: *Villa Bucci Verdicchio*

You're going to love the way the traditional collides with the creative in this innovative take on baked stuffed shrimp.

BOAT HOUSE

227 Schooner Drive
Tiverton, RI
401-624-6300
www.boathousetiverton.com

Chef: James Campagna

Owner: Starwood Tiverton, LLC

Cuisine: Waterfront dining

Specialty: A contemporary twist on the traditional seaside eatery, featuring fresh, local seafood, meats and organic produce.

Signature dishes: Maine lobster; mussels steamed in wine; grilled Block Island swordfish

Price range: Appetizers, $5 to $15

Entrees, $14 to $28

Hours: Open seven days a week

Monday to Thursday, 11:30 am to 9 pm

Friday and Saturday, 11:30 am to 10 pm

Sunday, 11 am to 9 pm with brunch from 11 am to 2 pm

CORN AND CRAB BAKED STUFFED SHRIMP
(12 servings)

1/2 cup unsalted butter
1 onion, finely diced
1 carrot, finely diced
1 jalapeño, finely diced
1 red pepper, finely diced
½ bunch celery, finely diced
1 tablespoon chopped garlic
1 cup sour cream
2 cups corn, roasted
1 tablespoon herbs
1 tablespoon honey
¼ cup lemon juice
1 to 2 cups bread crumbs
2 tablespoons Old Bay Seasoning
3 cups Jonah crabmeat
3 pounds Mexican white shrimp, large enough for stuffing

Preheat oven to 375 degrees.

In a frying pan, melt the butter over medium heat. Add the onions, carrots, peppers, celery and garlic, and cook until translucent. Remove from heat, and fold the sour cream into the mix. Fold in the remaining ingredients, except the shrimp, lightly folding in the crabmeat last. Set aside to cool. Butterfly the shrimp. Divide the stuffing into 2-ounce portions. Stuff each shrimp, folding the tail over the top. Place the stuffed shrimp in a baking dish. Bake in the 375-degree oven for 10 to 12 minutes. Serve immediately.

Recommended wine: *Chateau Souverain Chardonnay*

BON CALDO

1381 Boston Providence Hwy
Norwood, MA
781-255-5800
www.BonCaldo.com

Chef: Adam Laliberte

Owners: Joe and Frank Boncaldo

Cuisine: Regional Italian

Specialty: Fresh pasta

Signature dish: Chianti Wine
Braised Short Ribs

Price range: Appetizers,
$7 to $12

Entrees,
$13 to $34

Hours: Open seven days a week

Monday through Thursday,
11:30 am to 10 pm

Friday and Saturday,
11:30 am to 11 pm

Sunday,
noon to 9 pm

They'll melt in your mouth! Don't forget to save a little Chianti for your glass.

CHIANTI WINE BRAISED BONELESS BEEF SHORT RIBS
(4 servings)

5 pounds boneless beef short ribs
Salt and pepper, to taste
2 yellow onions, chopped
2 carrots, chopped
2 celery stalks, chopped
1 bottle Chianti wine
2 quarts beef or veal stock
1 cup crushed tomatoes
1 tablespoon fresh oregano

Preheat oven to 325 degrees.

Season the short ribs with salt and pepper. In a large skillet, brown all the ribs over high heat. Place the browned ribs in a large Dutch oven or oven-proof casserole dish. Sauté the vegetables in the fat rendered by the ribs until tender. Add the wine and simmer until reduced by half. Add the stock, crushed tomatoes and oregano, and bring to a boil. Pour the hot liquid mixture over the ribs. Cover with a lid or aluminum foil, and braise in the 325-degree oven for 3 to 4 hours. When the ribs are tender, reduce the sauce until it starts to thicken. Serve with creamy polenta, mashed potatoes, or buttered pasta.

Recommended wine: *Castello di Rampolla Chianti Classico*

You'll need bread for dippin' and wine for sippin' with this zesty classic.

BRICK ALLEY PUB & RESTAURANT

140 Thames Street
Newport, RI
401-849-6334
www.brickalley.com

CLAMS PORTUGUESE
(4 servings)

1 pound Portuguese chorizo sausage, casings removed, coarsely crumbled
2 large white onions, halved, thinly cut cross-wise into ⅓-inch thick slices
2 large green bell peppers, cut into ⅓-inch thick slices
2 (8-ounce) bottles clam juice
1 cup dry white wine
¼ teaspoon dried crushed red pepper (or more if sausage is mild)
32 littleneck clams (about 5 pounds), scrubbed
¾ cup chopped fresh cilantro, divided
1 red bell pepper, finely chopped
1 lemon, cut into 8 wedges

Heat a large pot over medium-high heat. Add first 3 ingredients to pot; sauté until vegetables are tender and sausage is brown, stirring frequently and breaking up the sausage with the back of a fork, about 10 minutes. Add the clam juice, wine and crushed red pepper; bring to a boil. Reduce heat to medium; simmer 3 minutes. Add clams; cover and cook until clams open, about 8 minutes. Discard any clams that do not open. Stir in ½ cup cilantro.

Transfer contents of pot to a very large bowl. Top with remaining cilantro and chopped red pepper. Garnish with lemon wedges.

Recommended wine: *Nessa Albarino*

Chefs:	Executive Chef Ralph H. Plumb Jr.
	and Chef Gary Mathias
Owners:	Ralph and Pat Plumb
Cuisine:	American
Specialty:	Steak and seafood
Signature dish:	Newport Cioppino
Price range:	Appetizers, $8 to $14
	Entrees, $17 to $29
Hours:	Open seven days a week
	Monday to Saturday, 11:30 am to 10 pm
	Sunday, 10:30 am to 10 pm

CAFÉ FRESCO

301 Main Street
East Greenwich, RI
401-398-0027
www.cafefrescori.com

Chef: Tony Morales

Owners: Jack Walrond
          and Tony Morales

Cuisine: Northern Italian/
          American

Specialty: A comfortable dining
          experience with a
          made-to-order menu
          that uses only the
          freshest ingredients expertly
          prepared and offered
          with friendly service.

Price range: Appetizers,
          $6 to $12

          Entrees,
          $12 to $20

Hours: Open every day of the
          week at 5 pm for dinner.

Whether you enjoy this duck creation "al fresco" or "inside," it is delicious, like everything else at this incredible East Greenwich restaurant.

AL FRESCO DUCK

(2 servings)

1 and ½ cups Muscat or other dessert wine, divided
1 and ½ cups low-salt chicken broth, divided
4 green shallots or scallions, chopped
3 garlic cloves, flattened
1 and ½ tablespoons Dijon mustard
1 tablespoon Worcestershire sauce
6 small boneless duck breast halves, approximately 2 pounds total
Salt and pepper, to taste
2 and ½ tablespoons butter

In a large bowl, combine ½ cup wine, ¼ cup broth, shallots, garlic, mustard and Worcestershire sauce. Place the duck breasts in the bowl, and marinate for 20 minutes.

Heat a large skillet over medium-high heat. Remove the duck breasts from the bowl, and reserve the marinade. Season the duck with salt and pepper, then place the duck breasts skin side down in the skillet. Cook until the skin is brown, approximately 5 minutes. Reduce heat to medium. Turn the duck breasts over. Cook to desired doneness, up to 10 minutes.

Place the duck breasts on a large plate. To the skillet add the remaining wine, broth, ⅓ cup of the marinade, and butter. Bring to a boil, whisking often, until the liquids are reduced to about ¾ cup, about 10 to 15 minutes. Serve the duck breasts with this sauce.

Chef's note: At Café Fresco, we serve this with black beans flavored with onions, garlic, bacon, cilantro, cumin, and more of that sweet dessert wine.

Recommended wine: *Erath Pinot Noir*

So, maybe you don't have a WaterFire and gondola rides outside your window like they do...but now you do have a signature recipe from one of Rhode Island's premier restaurants.

BOUILLABAISSE WITH ROUILLE

(4 servings)

Broth:

- ¼ cup olive oil
- 1 tablespoon chopped garlic
- 4 cups chopped leeks
- 2 cans (3 pounds) plum tomatoes
- 2 cups white wine
- 1 and ½ teaspoons fennel seeds
- 1 teaspoon saffron
- 4 cups clam juice
- 3 cups water
- ¼ cup pernod
- Orange peel, parsley sprig, thyme sprig and 10 black peppercorns tied up in a cheesecloth bundle

Suggested Fish:

- 24 mussels
- 32 littleneck clams
- 16 large shrimp (U-10 are recommended)
- 16 large scallops
- 1 pound fresh fish
- 1 pound calamari

Rouille:

- ½ cup diced Idaho potatoes
- 1 tablespoon chopped garlic
- 2 tablespoons chopped cherry peppers
- ½ cup broth (from above)
- 1 teaspoon saffron
- 2 egg yolks
- ½ cup olive oil
- Pinch of salt
- Dash of white pepper

In a large, heavy-bottomed pot with a lid, heat the olive oil. Add the garlic and cook until golden brown over moderate heat. Add the leeks. Lower the heat, and sweat the leeks until they are soft, about 10 minutes.

Separate the pulp of the tomatoes from the juices, reserving the juices and rough chopping the pulp. Add the tomato pulp to the pot. Cover and cook for 5 minutes. Uncover, add the wine, and simmer for 15 minutes. Add the remaining ingredients and the reserved juices. Simmer for 40 minutes. Add the seafood, cover, and cook until the seafood is done, about 10 minutes.

To make the rouille, first cook the potatoes in lightly salted, boiling water until soft. Drain the potatoes, and transfer the potatoes into the bowl of a food processor. Add the chopped garlic, cherry peppers, broth, saffron, and egg yolks. Turn on the food processor, and process until smooth. Then drizzle in the olive oil. Season with salt and pepper.

Chef's note: Bouillabaisse is traditionally served in a bowl over French bread seasoned with a garlic aioli called rouille.

Recommended wine: *Domaine Ste Michelle Blanc de Blanc*

page 31

CAFÉ ROMANZO

495 Washington Street
Coventry, RI
401-821-8720
www.caferomanzo.com

Chef: Kevin Duffney

Owners: Kevin Duffney
and Jeff Stevenin

Cuisine: Creative American

Specialty: Game dishes

Signature dish: Stuffed Pumpkin
with Saffron Cream

Price range: Appetizers,
$6 to $10

Entrees,
$12 to $30

Hours: Tuesday through Thursday,
5 to 9 pm

Friday and Saturday,
5 to 10 pm

Sunday brunch,
10 am to 2 pm

This recipe is no trick and all treat!

SCALLOP STUFFED PUMPKINS WITH SAFFRON CREAM
(6 servings)

6 small sugar pumpkins
Olive oil, as needed
1 to 2 tablespoons butter
30 sea scallops
4 ounces (½ cup) Captain Morgan Spiced Rum
6 tablespoons brown sugar
Salt and pepper, to taste
½ cup sun-dried cranberries
2 cups baby spinach
3 cups cubed focaccia bread
1 cup white wine
1 shallot, chopped
Pinch of saffron
Freshly chopped thyme, rosemary and sage, as needed
1 and ½ cups heavy cream

Preheat oven to 400 degrees. Wash the pumpkins to remove any dirt, then pat dry. Place the pumpkins on a rack on a baking sheet, then lightly coat the pumpkins with oil. Bake for 30 to 45 minutes, until just soft to the touch. When the pumpkins are cool enough to handle, cut off the top of the pumpkins about ¼ of the way down. Scoop out the seeds and some of the flesh, and reserve. Rinse the seeds to remove any pulp and dry. Lightly coat the seeds with oil, then season with salt and pepper. Bake the seeds on a sheet pan, mixing them occasionally until brown, about 15 minutes.

In a large frying pan over medium-high heat, combine some olive oil and butter. When hot, sauté the scallops until brown. Add the rum, brown sugar, salt, pepper, cranberries, spinach and reserved pumpkin flesh. Cook until spinach wilts. Add the focaccia, toss to absorb any liquid, and remove from heat. Evenly distribute the mixture into the 6 pumpkins. Place the pumpkins back in the oven to keep them warm.

In a small saucepan, combine the white wine, shallots, saffron, herbs, salt and pepper. Simmer until most of the liquid is gone. Add the cream and reduce until thick. Strain and pour the sauce over each pumpkin. Garnish with pumpkin seeds and serve immediately.

Recommended wine: *Chateau Monfort Vouvray*

How can a creature that eats tin cans be responsible for such a delicious cheese?
A very tasty sandwich!

BEET AND GOAT CHEESE SANDWICHES

(4 servings)

1 bunch fresh beets
Olive oil, as needed
12 ounces fresh goat cheese
Salt and pepper, to taste
1 teaspoon herbes de Provence
3 fresh parsley sprigs
3 fresh thyme sprigs
6 garlic cloves, peeled
1 cup grapeseed oil
12 shelled walnuts
2 tablespoons walnut oil
4 ounces (¼ pound) mixed salad greens (mesclun)
1 teaspoon fresh lemon juice
Freshly ground black pepper

Preheat oven to 375 degrees.

Wash the beets. Cut off the stems, leaving about an inch attached to the beet. Lightly coat the beets with olive oil. Place them in a small baking pan with ¼ cup water. Cover the pan with aluminum foil. Bake for 1 to 2 hours, depending on the size of the beets. When done, a parking knife will pierce the beets with no resistance. Let the beets cool slightly, and peel them while still warm. Cover and refrigerate. This may be done several days in advance.

Cut the goat cheese into 12 equal pieces, and form each piece into a ball. Toss the balls with the herbs, garlic and grapeseed oil. Season with salt and pepper. Place in a covered jar and marinate overnight in the refrigerator.

When ready to serve, cut the beets into ¼-inch slices. Place a ball of goat cheese on a beet slice, and top with another beet slice, pressing down just slightly to make a sandwich. Arrange the beet sandwiches on individual salad plates, and top each sandwich with a walnut and a drizzle of walnut oil. Toss the salad greens with enough walnut oil and lemon juice to suit your taste. Season with salt and pepper. Place a small amount of greens on each plate. Sprinkle with a little freshly ground black pepper. Serve immediately.

In English, Dolce Vita means the Sweet Life.

SWEET POTATO PANCETTA HASH

(4 servings)

½ pound pancetta, cut into small dice
½ pound white onions, cut into small dice
1 pound sweet potatoes, peeled and cut into small dice
5 large fresh sage leaves, cut into very thin strips
Salt and pepper, to taste

In a large frying pan, cook pancetta over low heat until fat in rendered and pancetta begins to brown. Add onions and cook until almost translucent. Add sweet potatoes and sage, and cook until tender, approximately 30 minutes. Season with salt and pepper to taste.

Note: Pancetta is Italian bacon and available in Italian food markets.

Chef: Gianfranco Campanella

Owner: Gianfranco Marrocco

Cuisine: Authentic Italian
with a contemporary twist

Price range: Appetizers,
$2 to $11

Entrees,
$6 to $18

Hours: Open seven days
a week for breakfast,
lunch, dinner and
late-night fare,
plus brunch on weekends.

Sunday through Thursday,
7:30 am to 1 am

Friday and Saturday,
7:30 am to 2 am

CAFFE DOLCE VITA

Authentic Italian Caffe

In English, it also means wow! Want to perk up your brunch?

CAMILLE'S

71 Bradford Street
Providence, RI
401-751-4812
www.camillesonthehill.com

Chef: John Granata

Owner: Top of the Hill LLC

Cuisine: Classical and
            contemporary Italian

Specialty: Seafood,
         prime steaks and veal

Signature dish: Pan-fried
                Veal Chop

Price range: Appetizers,
                $10 to $18

              Entrees,
            $20 to $40

Hours: Monday through Thursday,
         11:30 am to 10 pm

              Friday,
         11:30 am to 11 pm

              Saturday,
              5 to 11 pm

Camille's no longer has the intimate alcoves that surrounded the dining room, but they still have fabulous food.

PAN-FRIED VEAL CHOPS
(2 servings)

2 (16-ounce) veal chops
2 eggs
¼ cup milk
1 cup plain breadcrumbs
½ cup panko breadcrumbs
1 cup flour
1 cup olive oil
2 cups fresh tomato sauce
2 slices prosciutto di Parma
2 slices buffalo mozzarella

Lightly pound the veal to make it more tender. In one bowl, whip together the eggs and milk. In a second bowl, combine the plain and panko breadcrumbs. Place the flour in a third bowl. Dredge the veal in the flour, then in the egg mixture, and then in the breadcrumb mixture.

Preheat oven to 425 degrees.

In a large frying pan, heat the oil to 325 degrees. Fry the veal chops until golden brown. Lay both chops on a baking sheet pan. Cover the chops with tomato sauce, then the prosciutto, then the cheese. Place the sheet pan in the 425-degree oven, and bake until the cheese is melting slightly, about 5 minutes. Serve immediately.

Chef's note: This goes well with linguine pasta in pink vodka sauce.

Recommended wine: *Luigi Einaudi Barolo*

In a word.... luscious! We used the leftover sauce to marinate chicken which we grilled over a real wood fire. Our guests were raving about the unique taste.

CHIMICHURRI SAUCE

1 and ½ cups olive oil
6 tablespoons sherry wine vinegar or red wine vinegar
6 tablespoons fresh lemon juice
6 garlic cloves, peeled
4 medium shallots, peeled, quartered
2 teaspoons fine sea salt
1 teaspoon freshly ground pepper
1 teaspoon dried crushed red pepper
6 cups (packed) stemmed fresh parsley
4 cups (packed) stemmed fresh cilantro
2 cups (packed) stemmed fresh mint

Combine the first 8 ingredients in a blender; blend until almost smooth. Add ¼ of the parsley, ¼ of the cilantro, and ¼ of the mint; blend until incorporated. Add remaining herbs in 3 more additions, pureeing until almost smooth after each addition.

Chef's note: This is an excellent sauce to serve with steaks.

CAPRICCIO

2 Pine Street
Providence, RI
401-421-1320
www.capriccios.com

Chef: Nino D'Urso

Owner: Vincenzo Iemma

Cuisine: Fine European with a Northern Italian Accent

Specialty: Tableside flambé dishes

Signature dish: Dover Sole

Price range: Appetizers, $5 to $19

Entrees, $21 to $63

Hours: Lunch on Monday through Friday, 11:30 am to 3 pm

Dinner on Monday through Thursday, 5 to 10:30 pm; Friday and Saturday, 4 to 11 pm; and Sunday, 4 to 9 pm

Take a bow... Now you'll be able to tell everyone that you can cook just like the Master Chef Nino D'Urso!

MEDALLIONS OF BEEF TENDERLOIN WITH PORCINI AND MARSALA SAUCE

(6 servings)

12 beef tenderloin medallions, 2 and ½ ounces each
Salt and black pepper, to taste
8 tablespoons clarified butter
3 tablespoons finely chopped shallots
6 ounces (¾ cup) fresh or frozen porcini mushrooms
1 cup dry red wine
½ cup dry Marsala wine
6 tablespoons beef stock
1 and ½ cups heavy cream, reduced to ¾ cup

Season the beef tenderloin medallions with salt and pepper. In a large skillet, heat the butter over medium-high heat. Sauté the medallions in the skillet to the desired degree of doneness. Remove the medallions from the pan, and keep them warm on a heated serving plate.

Add the shallots and porcini mushrooms to the skillet. Sauté for several minutes. Add the red wine and Marsala wine. Continue cooking until the wines are almost completely reduced. Add the beef stock. Stir in the cream. Taste the sauce, and adjust the seasoning. Spoon the sauce over the meat.

Chef's note: Asparagus or glazed oven-roasted carrots are suggested as accompaniments to this dish.

Recommended wine: *DeForville Barbaresco*

Ah, simply an Italian classic. Psst... "pomodoro" means tomato in Italian.

PASTA POMODORO
(4 servings)

¼ cup olive oil
2 tablespoons sliced garlic
4 roasted garlic cloves
1 ounce proscuitto, cut into thin julienne strips
1 bay leaf
½ cup white wine
1 (16-ounce) can Italian peeled tomatoes
2 tablespoons chopped parsley
10 basil leaves, chopped
12 ounces linguine pasta
Salt and pepper, to taste

In a hot sauté pan, heat the olive oil. Add the sliced garlic and roasted garlic to the pan. Cook until the sliced garlic is lightly caramelized. Add the proscuitto and bay leaf, cook lightly, and deglaze the pan with the white wine. Add the Italian tomatoes, half of the parsley, and half of the basil.

In a pot of boiling salted water, cook the pasta until al dente, drain, and place on a warm pasta platter. Season the sauce with salt and pepper. Add the remaining fresh herbs to the sauce. Ladle the sauce on top of the pasta. Serve immediately.

Chef's note: To roast the garlic, peel the 4 cloves and coat them with some olive oil. Place the garlic cloves in a baking dish. Bake in a preheated 350-degree oven for 30 to 45 minutes, depending on the size of the garlic cloves.

Recommended wine: *Monte Antico Rosso Toscana*

CASTLE HILL INN & RESORT

590 Ocean Drive
Newport, RI
401-849-3800
www.castlehillinn.com

Chef: Jonathan Cambra

Owner: Newport Harbor Group

Cuisine: Original modern American

Specialty: Strong focus on regional ingredients in season

Price range: Prix-fixe menu:
3 courses, $65;
5 courses, $75;
8 courses, $85

Hours: Open seven days a week

Lunch on
Monday through Saturday,
starting at 11:30 am

Dinner on
Sunday through Thursday,
6 to 9 pm;
Friday and Saturday,
6 to 10 pm

Sunday brunch,
11:30 am to 3 pm

The dining room in this stunning waterfront resort is pristine, complementing dishes at this culinary level.

GRILLED NATIVE STRIPED BASS, WITH ORGANIC HEIRLOOM TOMATO RELISH

(4 servings)

32 ounces boneless, skinless, trimmed striped bass (8 ounces per person)
Olive oil, as needed
Kosher salt and white pepper, to taste
8 cups organic field greens
1 cup extra virgin olive oil
¼ cup lemon juice
1 tablespoon minced jalapenos
1 teaspoon minced shallots
2 cups diced heirloom tomatoes
½ cup extra virgin olive oil
1 tablespoon minced jalapenos
¼ cup minced shallots
1 tablespoon minced garlic
1 bunch fresh basil

Preheat the grill. Rub the fish with olive oil to prevent from sticking. Season the fish with salt and pepper. Place the fish on the grill, presentation side down first. Grill each side for approximately 4 minutes.

Toss the greens with next four ingredients. Season with salt and pepper right before the dish is served. Toss the diced tomatoes with the next four ingredients. Season with salt and pepper.

Clean and wash the basil. Puree in blender with just enough olive oil until you have a smooth mixture. Season to taste with salt and pepper.

To assemble, place the dressed greens on a plate, top with the grilled fish, and garnish with the tomato relish. Drizzle a little basil oil around the plate for a garnish and for added taste.

Recommended wine: *Dog Point Sauvignon Blanc*

Exploring the exciting world of wine with...

Mark Gasbarro,
owner of Gasbarro's Wines on Federal Hill in Providence

CAV

14 Imperial Place
Providence, RI
401-751-9164
www.cavrestaurant.com

Chefs: Chow Malakorn
and Neil Roy

Owner: Sylvia Moubayed

Cuisine: Upscale contemporary

Specialty: Creative twists
on classic principles

Price range: Appetizers
(enough for two people to share),
$7 to $14

Entrees,
$14 to $30

A special bistro menu
is offered Sunday through
Thursday, priced at $16.95.

Hours: Open seven days
a week for lunch
and dinner with brunch
on Saturday and Sunday

Monday through Friday,
11:30 am to 10 pm

Friday,
11:30 am to 1 am

Saturday,
10 am to 1 am

Sunday,
10 am to 10 pm

For the discerning lover of seafood.

SCALLOPS WITH BALSAMIC REDUCTION AND LOBSTER BUTTER
(2 servings)

2 tablespoons olive oil
8 jumbo diver sea scallops (U-10 are recommended)
Salt and pepper, to taste

Balsamic Reduction:
    2 cups aged Modena balsamic vinegar
    4 tablespoons sugar

Lobster Butter:
    3 lobster bodies
    1 and ½ pounds butter (6 sticks), divided
    3 tablespoons tomato paste
    ½ teaspoon paprika

Chef's note: Both the balsamic reduction and lobster butter may be prepared in advance and kept in the refrigerator. You can use these wonderful sauces in many other dishes.

In a saucepan over medium-high heat, add the olive oil. Season the scallops with salt and pepper. Pan sear the scallops until golden brown on both sides and still medium rare on the inside.

In a sauté pan over medium heat, combine the balsamic vinegar and sugar. Bring to a boil, stirring to dissolve the sugar, then reduce to a simmer. Reduce until slightly thickened.

In a large saucepan over medium heat, combine the lobster bodies and 2 tablespoons of butter. Cook for 5 minutes. Crush the bodies. Add the tomato paste and paprika. Cook for 5 more minutes. Add the remaining butter, and turn up the heat to medium-high to clarify the butter. Strain into a container through cheesecloth.

Plate the scallops with some of the lobster butter in a semi-circle, and then some of the balsamic reduction. With a toothpick, streak the two sauces vertically to create a design.

Chef's note: At CAV, these scallops are served over Lemon Zest Risotto, topped with two intertwined grilled shrimp and julienned snow peas that have been lightly sautéed in butter.

Recommended wine: *Terre Rouge Roussane*

Like CAV, this dish needs to be savored.

CILANTRO MEXICAN GRILL

127 Weybosset Street
Providence, RI
401-421-8226
www.cilantromex.com

Once you try it, you'll know why Kate's braggin'.

KATE'S GREAT CORN MANGO SALSA
(8 servings)

40 ounces (5 cups) kernel corn
1 and ⅓ cups diced red onions
¼ cup diced jalapeno peppers
⅛ cup fresh lime juice
2 teaspoons kosher salt
½ cup diced fresh mango

In a very large mixing bowl, combine the corn, red onions, jalapeno peppers, and fresh lime juice. Sprinkle the salt evenly over the contents of the entire bowl. Add the diced mango. Mix gently with a large rubber spatula. Serve immediately. Cover and refrigerate any leftover salsa.

Owner: John Palmieri

Cuisine: California-style
                    Mexican

Specialty: Fresh salsas

Signature dish: Giant Chicken
                    Burrito

Price range: Appetizers,
                    $4

                    Entrees,
                    $7

Hours: Open seven days a week,
        11 am to 10 pm

A cutting-edge recipe from a trendy downcity hot spot.

OLIVE OIL POACHED SALMON WITH APRICOT-GINGER SAUCE
(4 servings)

1 tablespoon minced fresh ginger
1 quart extra virgin olive oil
2 ounces (¼ cup) sake (rice wine)
1 quart apricot puree
4 wild King salmon filets, 8 ounces each
8 heads baby bok choy
Salt and pepper, to taste
1 teaspoon sriracha (red chili sauce)

To make the sauce, in a large frying pan, sauté the minced ginger in a tablespoon of olive oil until slightly brown. Deglaze the pan with sake. Add the apricot puree, bring to a boil, strain and cool. Set aside.

In a large saucepan over low heat (ideal temperature is around 200 degrees), heat the remaining olive oil. Submerge the salmon filets for about 6 minutes for medium doneness, up to 9 minutes for well done. Remove salmon filets from the oil. Set aside on a warm platter.

While the salmon is cooking, cut each head of bok choy in half. Place the bok choy in boiling water for 1 minute. Remove the bok choy from the water, then sauté the bok choy in butter in a large frying pan. Season with salt and pepper.

To serve, place the bok choy on a plate with the salmon filet on top. Pour the sauce around the salmon using a spoon or squeeze bottle. Add a little sriracha for heat and color.

Recommended wine: *Trimbach Gewurtztraminer*

CITRON WINE BAR & BISTRO

5 Memorial Boulevard
Providence, RI
401-621-9463
www.citronri.com

Chefs:	Executive Chef Nick Rabar
	Chef de Cuisine Matt Foley
Owners:	John Elkhay, Rick and Cheryl Bready
Cuisine:	American Bistro
Signature dish:	Ahi Tuna Tasting
Price range:	Appetizers, $5.50 to $12
	Entrees, $16 to $25
Hours:	Open seven days a week
	Sunday brunch, 10:30 am to 2:30 pm
	Lunch, Monday through Friday, 11:30 am to 2:30 pm
	Dinner, every night, 4:30 pm to closing
	Late-night menu, Sunday through Thursday, 10 to 11 pm; Friday and Saturday, 11 pm to 1 am

Chef Alberto's incredible creation is wha

ZUPPA DI ZUCCA (BRAISED PUMPKIN SOUP)

(4 to 6 servings)

For the soup:
I medium-size pumpkin, peeled and cut into ½-inch cubes
I medium-size Spanish onion
2 carrots, peeled and cut into ¼-inch slices
I stick (8 tablespoons) unsalted butter
2 tablespoons brown sugar
½ teaspoon ground nutmeg
3 tablespoons honey
I quart milk
I cup heavy cream
Salt and pepper, to taste

For the garnish:
Thin slices of day-old bread and roasted pumpkin seed oil

Preheat oven to 375 degrees.

In a large casserole dish, combine the diced pumpkin, onions, carrots and butter. Cover with aluminum foil and bake for about 20 minutes, or until the pumpkin and carrots are soft and the onions are translucent.

In a large saucepan, combine the remaining ingredients, mixing well. Bring just to a boil, then reduce heat and simmer for 15 minutes. Add the baked pumpkin mixture to the saucepan.

With a food processor or blender, puree the soup in small batches to get a smooth texture. Season to taste with salt and pepper.

Garnish each bowl of soup with a thin slice of day-old bread that is topped with fresh goat cheese and a drizzle of roasted pumpkin seed oil. Serve immediately.

Chef Alberto

I like to call a lesson in "the art of soup."

Remember, veal scallopine is tender and thin and shouldn't be overcooked. Now put a little 'zingarella' in your life.

VEAL ZINGARELLA
(4 servings)

Flour, as needed for dusting
1 pound veal scaloppini
Salt and pepper, to taste
Olive oil, as needed
2 tablespoons butter, divided
1 small onion, thinly sliced
1 bell pepper, thinly sliced
4 garlic cloves, chopped
1 (14-ounce) can plum tomatoes, crushed by hand
6 ounces (¾ cup) roasted peppers, drained and cut into thin julienne strips
⅛ cup hot pepper rings, with its juice
1 small can (6 ounces) tomato paste
2 tablespoons torn (not chopped) fresh basil
Crushed red pepper flakes, to taste

Flour the veal on both sides. Season with salt and pepper. In a large frying pan, sauté the veal in a little bit of oil until lightly cooked on both sides. Remove the veal from the pan. Set aside on a plate covered with a paper towel.

Drain the oil from the pan. Add 1 tablespoon of butter to the pan over medium-high heat. Add the onions, bell pepper and garlic. Cook until the onions are tender. Add the tomatoes, roasted peppers and hot pepper rings. Simmer for 10 minutes. Add tomato paste and fresh basil. Check the taste. Add salt, pepper and crushed red pepper flakes, to taste. Place the veal back in the pan to warm through, then serve immediately.

Chef's note: This is great with roasted potatoes or over pasta.

Recommended wine: *Amano Primitivo*

A tasty treat from this suburban hotspot that offers
"big city food and ambiance without the big city price tag."

SEVEN-HOUR BRAISED BEEF SHORT RIBS
(4 servings)

4 cups canola oil
4 cups diced Spanish onions
1 and ½ cups diced celery
1 and ½ cups diced carrots
5 garlic cloves, sliced
4 cups red wine
4 ounces (½ cup) tomato paste
8 short ribs, 8 ounces each approximately
6 cups chicken stock
Salt and pepper, to taste

In a medium-size saucepan, heat 1 cup of oil over medium-high heat. Add the onions, and cook for 2 to 3 minutes, stirring occasionally. Add the celery, carrots and garlic. Cook until the vegetables start to brown. Add the wine. Allow the wine to reduce by about one-quarter. Add the tomato paste, stirring to fully incorporate into the sauce. Reduce heat to low and cook for another 10 minutes, or until sauce has fully thickened.

Preheat oven to 250 degrees. Pour the remaining oil into a sauté pan with high sides over high heat. Season both sides of the short ribs generously with salt and pepper. When the oil in the pan just starts to smoke, add the short ribs and sear on both sides, about 2 minutes or until golden brown. You may want to do this in batches. Do not overcrowd the pan.

Pour the sauce into a large roasting pan, and spread the sauce evenly across the bottom of the pan. Add the short ribs to the pan, bone side up. Add enough chicken stock to almost completely cover the short ribs. Cover the short ribs with parchment paper. Place the roasting pan into the 250-degree oven. Roast for about 7 hours, or until the meat is falling off the bone. When cooked, remove the short ribs from the pan. Strain the braising liquid and use this to sauce the short ribs, if desired.

Chef's note: You could serve mashed potatoes, pasta or risotto with these short ribs. At D. Carlo Trattoria, the short ribs are served with roasted creamer potatoes, baby leeks, baby carrots and red pearl onions.

Recommended wine: *Capezzana Carmignano*

DE WOLF TAVERN

259 Thames Street
Bristol, RI
401-254-2005
www.dewolftavern.com

Chef: Sai Viswanath

Owners: Miles Ave. Property Co.
          and Sai Viswanath

Cuisine: Contemporary American

Specialty: Lobster Popovers

Signature dish: Sweet Potato or
          Mushroom Gnocchi

Price range: Appetizers,
               $6 to $15

               Entrees,
               $18 to $29

Hours: Open seven days a week

               Monday to Saturday,
               5 to 10 pm

               Sunday brunch,
               10:30 am to 2:30 pm;

               Sunday dinner,
               5 to 9 pm

Does it get any better than homemade lobster popovers?
Let me answer that for you...no!

LOBSTER POPOVERS
(4 servings)

2 live lobsters, 1 and ¼ pounds each

For the popovers:
⅔ cup milk
1 large egg
1 teaspoon salt
6 tablespoons plus 1 teaspoon
    all-purpose flour
2 and ½ tablespoons Wondra flour

For the sauce:
2 tablespoons unsalted butter
6 medium shallots, minced
3 garlic cloves, minced
⅛ cup tomato paste
½ cup sherry
1 cup lobster or fish stock
2 tablespoons heavy cream
Salt, to taste
Freshly ground black pepper, to taste
    (Tellicherry, if available)

Drop the lobsters into boiling salted water and cook for 7 minutes. Remove from the water and drain. When cool enough to handle, crack the shells and remove the meat. Cut meat into 1-inch pieces and drain well.

While the lobsters are cooking, prepare the popovers. Whisk together the milk and egg. Combine the salt and both flours. Spray the popover pan with nonstick oil spray.

Add the milk mixture to the dry mixture, and blend until just combined. Spoon the batter into the popover pan, filling each cup no more than half full. Place the pan into a cold oven. Turn the heat to 375 degrees and cook until browned and puffed, about 25 to 35 minutes.

Prepare the sauce by melting the butter in a medium-size saucepan. Add the shallots and garlic. Cook over medium heat, stirring often, until caramelized. Add the tomato paste and continue cooking and stirring until the paste is caramelized as well.

Add the sherry and stock. Whisk to combine. Finish with the cream, salt and pepper. Cook the sauce until it reaches a light consistency. Warm the lobster meat in the sauce. To serve, cut a warm popover in half. Place the cut side up on a plate and spoon the lobster meat and sauce into the popover. If desired, serve with a small mesclun salad.

Recommended wine: *Mandarossa Fiano*

Welcoming celebrities to Providence...

Jed Steele, renowned California winemaker

Coach Don Shula, Shula's 347 Grille

Mary Ann Esposito, television celebrity chef
and cookbook author

Nancy Verde Barr, author and expert
on Italian food and wine

ELEVEN FORTY NINE

1149 Division Street
Warwick, RI
401-884-1149
www.eleven49.com

Chef:	Jules Ramos
Owners:	Tom Wright and John Picerne
Cuisine:	New American
Specialty:	Local products
Price range:	Appetizers, $6 to $12
	Entrees, $7 to $39
Hours:	Lunch, Monday through Saturday, 11:30 am to 3:30 pm
	Dinner, Monday through Thursday, 5 to 10 pm; Friday and Saturday, 5 to 11 pm.
	Sunday, 2 to 8 pm

Thanks to Chef Jules Ramos, you can now say

MEATBALL SLIDERS
(4 servings)

Meatballs:

2 tablespoons extra virgin olive oil
1 large onion, diced small
3 garlic cloves, minced
½ pound ground veal
½ pound ground pork
½ pound ground beef
¼ cup ketchup
¼ cup finely chopped parsley
¼ cup finely chopped fresh basil
1 teaspoon dried oregano
2 cups fresh breadcrumbs or Panko bread crumbs
1 cup grated parmesan cheese
2 large eggs
Dash Worcestershire sauce
Salt and pepper, to taste

In a sauté pan over medium-high heat, add the oil. Cook the onions until golden brown. Allow to cool to room temperature. In a large mixing bowl, combine the remaining ingredients. Do not overwork because that will make the meatballs tough. It is also a good idea to make sure that all of the ingredients are cold prior to mixing. Season with salt and pepper. Place a small sauté pan over medium heat, and cook a small piece of the meatball mixture. Taste to make sure that the flavor profile is right. You might need to adjust the seasoning with a little more salt and pepper.

Preheat oven to 350 degrees.

Shape the meatballs with an ice cream scoop. Place them on a cookie sheet or baking sheet pan that has been coated with extra virgin olive oil. Roast the meatballs for 35 to 45 minutes in the 350-degree oven. The meatballs should be golden brown and cooked through. Add the meatballs to a big pot of "red gravy" and simmer for 2 hours at a very slow simmer. Use your favorite recipe to make the red gravy, or buy a jar of good quality marinara sauce.

Chef's note: If the gravy starts to get too thick, add a little water or chicken broth. Make sure that you stir the pot once in a while to keep it from sticking.

bye~bye to meatballs as you know them!

For the sliders:

    Mini rolls, slightly larger than the size of a meatball, as needed

    Grated parmesan cheese, as needed

    Fresh mozzarella, sliced thin, as needed

    Fresh basil leaves, as needed

Preheat the oven to 375 degrees. Place the cooked meatballs on a cookie sheet. Drizzle some red gravy over the meatballs, and sprinkle some parmesan cheese over the meatballs. Drape a slice of fresh mozzarella and a basil leaf over each meatball. Place the cookie sheet in the 375-degree oven, and bake just until the cheese melts. Put one meatball into a mini roll, and serve immediately.

Recommended wine: *Badiola Rossa Toscana*

Chiara is a beautiful name.
This dish is named in honor of Euro Bistro owner Ken Turchetta's daughter.

CHICKEN CHIARA
(4 servings)

4 boneless, skinless chicken breasts, cut into bite-size pieces, approximately 24 ounces
¼ cup olive oil
4 garlic cloves, minced
1 cup sherry
2 cups chicken stock
4 ounces (½ cup) roasted red peppers
4 ounces (½ cup) crimini mushrooms
4 ounces (½ cup) artichoke hearts
2 tablespoons butter
Salt and pepper, to taste
1 pound penne pasta, cooked

In a large frying pan, sauté the chicken in olive oil until golden brown on all sides. Add the garlic to the pan. Deglaze the pan with sherry wine and chicken stock. Add the roasted red peppers, mushrooms, artichoke hearts and butter. Continue to cook for 2 to 3 minutes. Season to taste with salt and pepper. In a large serving bowl, combine the chicken mixture with the cooked pasta. Serve immediately.

Recommended wine: *Scuarti Nero d'Avola*

Owner: Kenneth Turchetta

Cuisine: Italian American

Price range: Appetizers,
$9 to $13

Entrees,
$16 to $22

Hours: Monday through Thursday,
11:30 am to 9 pm

Friday,
11:30 am to 10 pm

Saturday,
5 to 10 pm

The chowder and clam cakes are excellent.
Make sure you get a slice of their blueberry pie when you visit this slice of Americana.

TRADITIONAL RHODE ISLAND CHOWDER
(4 servings)

1 and ¼ cups butter (2 and ½ sticks)
⅛ cup chopped onion
⅛ cup clam base
1 tablespoon salt
1 and ½ teaspoons pepper
¼ quart (1 cup) shucked clams, chopped
1 gallon cold water
4 bay leaves
12 cups peeled, diced potatoes
½ cup half-and-half, optional

In a large stockpot, combine all the ingredients except the potatoes and the half-and-half. Bring the mixture to a boil. Add the potatoes and cook until tender, about 20 minutes.

This can be served as is, without the half-and-half, for a traditional Rhode Island chowder. Or you can add the half-and-half to make a New England chowder.

Chef's note: Clam base is sold in small jars in the soup section of large supermarkets.

EVELYN'S NANAQUAKET DRIVE-IN

2335 Main Road
Tiverton, RI
401-265-2146,
or 401-624-3100
www.evelynsdrivein.com

Chefs/owners: Jane and
                       Domenic Bitto

Cuisine: Traditional Clam Shack

Specialty: Chowder and clamcakes,
               grilled scallops,
               lobster chow mein,
               grapenut pudding

Signature dish: Fish and Chips

Price range: Appetizers,
                      $3 to $13

                        Entrees,
                      $4 to $31

Hours: Open seven days a week

                 Monday to Thursday,
                 11:30 am to 8 pm

                 Friday to Sunday,
                 11:30 am to 8:30 pm
                 (and open until 9 pm
                 in the summer)

EVELYN'S VILLA & THE DANCING DOG TAVERN

272 Cowesett Avenue
West Warwick, RI
401-821-0060
www.evelynsvilla.com

Chefs: Michael Brunette and
Michael Eddington

Owners: Ernest Simas and
Catherine Brunette

Cuisine: American

Specialty: Marinated mushrooms
and prime rib

Signature dish: Grilled Sausage
Ragout

Price range: Appetizers,
$7 to $10

Entrees,
$10 to $22

Hours: Monday,
4 to 10 pm

Wednesday and Thursday,
11:30 am to 11:30 pm

Friday and Saturday,
11:30 am to 1 am

Sunday,
noon to 11 pm

Breakfast on Saturday and Sunday,
7 am to noon

All right, sausage ragout over, let's say, rigatoni with, let's say, a glass of hearty red wine, and let's say, crusty Italian bread... brings me back to Mom's kitchen. Thank Evelyn's Villa if your special memory matches mine!

SAUSAGE RAGOUT

(2 servings)

1 tablespoon olive oil
1 teaspoon chopped garlic
1 small red onion, sliced
6 ounces andouille sausage, sliced
4 ounces (½ cup) portabello mushrooms, marinated, grilled and sliced
4 ounces (½ cup) roasted red peppers, sliced
6 ounces (¾ cup) cooked spinach
½ cup Madeira wine
1 cup marinara sauce
1 cup demi glace (now available in the soup section of large supermarkets)
4 tablespoons butter, cut into cubes
1 pound linguine pasta
Chopped parsley, as needed
Grated parmesan cheese, as needed

In a large sauté pan, heat the olive oil. Add the garlic, onions and sausage. Cook over medium heat, stirring constantly, until garlic begins to brown and onions become soft. Add the mushrooms, peppers and spinach. Deglaze pan with the wine. Cook for 3 to 4 minutes until the wine begins to reduce. Add the marinara sauce and demi glace. Stir and cook for a few minutes until the sauce is hot. Swirl in the butter until melted. Remove the pan from heat.

Cook the pasta according to package directions. Strain the pasta. Place the pasta in a large serving bowl, and pour the sauce over the pasta. Using tongs, mix the pasta and sauce until thoroughly coated. Portion into serving bowls, and sprinkle with parsley and grated cheese. Serve with hot crusty garlic bread.

Recommended wine: *Tatone Montepulciano*

A fitting recipe from a great Irish pub.

GUINNESS BBQ WINGS

(4 servings)

Guinness BBQ Sauce:

2 cups Guinness
½ cup dark brown sugar
¼ teaspoon ground cayenne pepper
¼ tablespoon garlic powder
¼ tablespoon onion powder
1 quart Bullseye Original BBQ Sauce

3 pounds fresh chicken wings, with first and second joint
1 cup Frank's Red Hot Sauce

In a heavy-based pot, combine the Guinness and brown sugar on low heat. Reduce this mixture by half. Whisk in the remaining sauce ingredients, mixing well. Simmer on low heat for 10 additional minutes. Set aside.

In a large bowl, marinate the wings in Frank's Red Hot Sauce for 1 hour. Cook the wings on a large sheet pan in the 350-degree oven for 1 hour. Using a large bowl, toss the cooked wings with the Guinness BBQ Sauce, evenly coating each wing. Serve on a platter with fresh celery and bleu cheese dressing.

Chef's note: And don't forget to pour yourself a Guinness Stout.

FAIAL RESTAURANT & LOUNGE

970 Douglas Pike
Smithfield, RI
401-231-1100

Faial is the name of the town in the Azores that the owner and chef of this popular Smithfield restaurant are from.

SEAFOOD RICE
(16 to 20 servings)

1 small onion, diced finely
¼ pound butter (1 stick)
8 cups water
1 tablespoon clam base
1 small foil pack Sazon Goya
¼ teaspoon paprika
5 (6-ounce) boxes Near East Rice Pilaf
1 teaspoon white pepper
1 tablespoon garlic powder
1 pound bay scallops
¼ pound tiny shrimp
1 and ¼ pounds crabmeat
2 bay leaves

In a frying pan, sauté the onion in the butter. Transfer the cooked onions to a shallow roasting pan (approximately 21x13 inches in size). Set aside.

In a medium-size pan, combine the water, clam base, Sazon Goya, and paprika. Bring to a boil. Preheat oven to 400 degrees.

To the roasting pan, add the rice and the seasoning packets from each box. Add the pepper, garlic powder, scallops, shrimp, crabmeat, and bay leaves. Mix well. Add the boiling water-clam base mixture. Cover the pan with foil. Bake in a preheated 400-degree oven for 90 minutes. Serve immediately as a side dish. Cover and refrigerate any leftover rice.

Chef: Antonio Pereira

Owners: Joe and Emily Faria

Cuisine: Portuguese-American

Specialty: Fresh seafood

Signature dish: Baked Stuffed
                        Swordfish

Price range: Appetizers,
                        $9 to $15

                            Entrees,
                        $10 to $25

Hours: Open seven days a week

        Sunday through Thursday,
            11:30 am to 9 pm

            Friday and Saturday,
            11:30 am to 10 pm

This first-class steakhouse at Twin River is owned by retired NFL stars Fred Smerlas and Steve DeOssie... By the way, this is an all-pro recipe!

CRAB SOUFFLÉ
(2 servings)

6 slices white bread
8 ounces (1 cup) jumbo lump crabmeat
6 ounces (¾ cup) mayonnaise
2 tablespoons Dijon mustard
1 egg
1 tablespoon Tabasco sauce, more or less to taste
Salt and pepper, to taste

Preheat oven to 325 degrees.

Dice the bread into ¼-inch pieces and place in a large bowl. Place the lump crabmeat in a separate bowl. Add the mayonnaise, mustard, egg and Tabasco to the lump crabmeat. Mix well. Season to taste with salt and pepper. Combine the bread with crab mixture, and place in a crock or ovenproof casserole. Bake in the 325-degree oven for 20 minutes or until golden brown. Serve hot out of the oven with crackers such as Triscuits.

Recommended wine: *Sella & Mosca La Cala Vermentino*

I love this dish. It's quick, simple and creative

PASTA WITH SMOKED GOUDA ALFREDO SAUCE
(1 serving)

1 tablespoon butter
1 teaspoon minced garlic
1 teaspoon minced yellow onion
½ teaspoon flour
1 and ½ cups cream
1 ounce (2 tablespoons) shredded smoked gouda cheese
½ ounce (1 tablespoon) grated parmesan cheese
1 teaspoon chicken stock
Salt and pepper, to taste
Cooked pasta, your choice

In a sauté pan, melt the butter. Add the garlic, onion and flour. When soft, add the cream and chicken stock. Allow sauce to reduce and thicken. Remove from the heat. Add the cheeses, salt and pepper. Toss the sauce with cooked pasta pasta, approximately ¼ pound, mixing to coat well. Serve immediately.

Chef's note: This recipe can easily be doubled to serve two.

Recommended wine: *Rengo Amarone*

Geppetto's
Pizzeria
Home of the legendary Grilled Pizza

And the smoked gouda really makes it!

Chef: David Ashworth

Owner: Gian Carlo Iannuccilli

Cuisine: Authentic Italian

Specialty: Fresh pasta
            and grilled meats

Signature dish: Orecchiette con
            Spinaci e Salsice

Price range: Appetizers,
            $6 to $9

            Entrees,
            $12 to $25

Hours: Tuesday through Friday,
            4 to 10 pm

            Saturday,
            5 to 11 pm

Sunday and Monday, open for
private functions only or holidays

Take your first bite, close your eyes, and imagine

ORECCHIETTE CON SPINACI E SALSICE
(ORECCHIETTE PASTA WITH SPINACH AND SAUSAGE)

(2 to 4 servings)

½ pound orecchiette pasta
2 tablespoons chopped garlic cloves
8 tablespoons extra virgin olive oil, divided
10 ounces hot Italian sausage, crumbled
8 cherry tomatoes
2 cups chopped fresh spinach
1 pinch salt
4 ounces (½ cup) goat cheese, crumbled
4 ounces (½ cup) Parmigiano Reggiano cheese, grated

In a large pot of boiling salted water, cook the orecchiette pasta until al dente, approximately 8 minutes. Chef's note: Orecchiette is always better when cooked in chicken stock instead of water.

In a large frying pan, sauté the garlic in 2 tablespoons of the olive oil until slightly golden. Add the crumbled sausage and cook through. Drain the oil from the pan. Add the remaining olive oil along with the cherry tomatoes and spinach. Quickly sauté. Add the salt.

Drain the pasta and add it to the frying pan, along with the goat cheese and Parmigiano Reggiano cheese. Toss quickly and serve immediately.

Recommended wine: *Vietti Nebbiolo*

Gian Carlo's
r i s t o r a n t e

Chef David

...you're eating with friends on the Italian countryside. Mangia bene!

GRACIE'S

194 Washington Street
Providence, RI
401-272-7811
www.graciesprov.com

Chef: Joseph Hafner

Owner: Ellen Gracyalny

Cuisine: American

Specialty: Chef's tasting menu

Signature dish: Foie gras

Price range: Appetizers,
            $11 to $19

            Entrees,
            $23 to $38

Hours: Tuesday to Saturday,
            5 pm to closing

            Sunday,
            4 pm to closing

This restaurant has a way with incredible freshness, simplicity, and flavor.

ASPARAGUS SALAD WITH PARMESAN VINAIGRETTE
(6 to 8 servings)

Vinaigrette:
>   4 to 5 ounces high quality parmesan cheese
>   1 and ½ cups water
>   1 shallot, finely minced
>   Champagne or other quality white vinegar, as needed
>   Chopped herbs (optional)

Salad:
>   2 bunches large green asparagus
>   2 bunches white asparagus
>   Extra virgin olive oil, as needed
>   ¼ pound exotic mushrooms (oyster, lobster or morel are recommended)
>   ½ pound ramps, leeks or scallions, washed and trimmed
>   3 to 4 tablespoons minced red onion or shallot
>   Quail eggs (optional)
>   Cracked black pepper, to taste
>   Pea greens or sprouts, for garnish

Shave the parmesan into small sections. Combine the shaved parmesan and water in a small saucepan over medium heat. Bring to a simmer, but not a rolling boil. Stir a few times and simmer for 10 minutes. The parmesan should melt and create a milky liquid. Keep stirring. Strain the liquid and reserve. You should have about 1 cup of parmesan water. Add the minced shallot and about ¼ cup vinegar. If desired, you may also add other chopped herbs such as thyme, parsley or chives. Set the parmesan vinaigrette aside for now.

Bring a large pot of heavily salted water to a boil for blanching. Prepare a large bowl of ice water for the asparagus to be shocked after it is cooked. Trim and peel the ends of the asparagus. Dunk the asparagus into the boiling water for approximately 1 minute. This may be done in batches. Then remove the asparagus from the boiling water and place in the ice water to stop the cooking process. Drain and dry.

Preheat oven to 400 degrees.

Divide the blanched asparagus into piles on a nonstick baking sheet. You should create piles of 3 green and 3 white asparagus for each person. Coat the asparagus piles with extra virgin olive oil.

Bake the asparagus in the 400-degree oven until warmed through, about 5 minutes.

Slice the mushrooms into thin slices and quarters. Set aside. Chef's note: If you cannot find exotic mushrooms, portobello and white mushrooms will give a similar flavor at a fraction of the cost. If you are using leeks, they should be cut into thin julienne strips.

In a large skillet over medium heat, add enough oil to coat the pan. Sauté the mushrooms, ramps (leeks or scallions), and red onion (or shallots) until they begin to wilt. At this point, the pan may start to be dry. If the vegetables are not wilted, add a little bit more oil or some unsalted butter. When the vegetables are wilted, add the parmesan vinaigrette until the ramps and mushrooms are almost covered. Allow this mixture to simmer and reduce slightly.

At this point, you can add a few tiny quail eggs for garnish if you want to impress your guests. Crack the eggs in a bowl beforehand and carefully place them along the side of the pan in the liquid. When the eggs are cooked, you are ready to serve.

Prepare your salad plates by placing the asparagus in neat piles in the center of each plate. Divide the mushroom mixture evenly among each pile. Spoon the quail eggs over the top if you are using them. Spoon some of the remaining vinaigrette over the salads. Garnish with cracked black pepper and pea greens or sprouts.

Chef's note: If the vinaigrette is loose after you have prepared the plates, you can reduce it on the stove and add a little bit of butter to thicken before serving.

Gracie's

GREGG'S RESTAURANTS

1303 North Main Street
Providence, RI
401-831-5700

1359 Post Road
Warwick, RI
401-467-5700

1940 Pawtucket Avenue
East Providence, RI
401-438-5700

4120 Quaker Lane
North Kingstown, RI
401-294-5700

www.greggsusa.com

Chef: Steve Trabucco

Owner: Ted Fuller

Cuisine: American

Specialty: Desserts

Price range: Appetizers,
                    $2.50 to $10.50

                    Entrees,
                    $8 to $15

Hours: Open seven days a
          week in general from
          11:30 am to midnight.
          Check each location
          for specific hours.

Thanks to my friends at Gregg's for giving me one of their signature recipes.

PECAN PIE
(6 to 8 servings)

8 ounces (1 cup) brown sugar
¼ teaspoon salt
¼ teaspoon cinnamon
8 tablespoons butter, melted
8 eggs, beaten
1 teaspoon vanilla extract
2 cups corn syrup
8 ounces (1 cup) pecans
1 (11-inch) prepared pie crust

In a large bowl, combine the brown sugar, salt and cinnamon. Add the melted butter and mix well. Add the eggs and vanilla extract, mixing well. Add the corn syrup and mix well.

Preheat oven to 300 degrees.

Place the pecans into the prepared pie crust, then add the liquid mixture. Bake the pie in the 300-degree oven for 1 and ½ to 2 hours. Serve warm or at room temperature.

The reason this has been a "great place to meet and a great place to eat"
for years is due in large part to creative dishes like this one.

SHRIMP AND CHICKEN LO MEIN
(1 serving)

1 tablespoon sesame oil
4 ounces (½ cup) diced chicken
3 extra-large shrimp, tails off, cleaned and deveined
1 pinch ground ginger
1 cup wok vegetables (nappa cabbage, green peppers, carrots and celery)
¼ cup edamame
10 ounces (1 and ¼ cups) hoisin sauce
1 cup coconut milk
½ cup chicken stock
1 cup cooked lo mein noodles

In a large sauté pan, heat the oil. Pan sear the chicken until it is almost done. Add the shrimp
to the pan. Add the ginger, wok vegetables and edamame, tossing a couple of times to coat well.
Add the hoisin sauce, coconut milk and chicken stock. Continue cooking until reduced to a thick
sauce. Add the cooked lo mein noodles. Toss to coat well. Serve immediately.

Chef's note: It's very easy to double this recipe.

Recommended wine: *Pierre Sparr Riesling*

Aptly named... you'll hit the flavor jackpot with this simple yet tasty dish.

BAKED SCROD WITH CASINO BUTTER TOPPING
(4 servings)

2 pounds fresh scrod
Casino Butter Topping:
    1 medium green pepper
    1 medium red pepper
    1 medium onion
    1 tablespoon olive oil
    Salt and pepper, to taste
    ½ teaspoon chopped garlic
    ½ pound butter, at room temperature (2 sticks)
    3 to 4 dashes Tabasco sauce
    3 to 4 dashes Worcestershire sauce
    ¼ cup gin
    ¼ cup anisette
    1 cup crushed Ritz crackers
½ cup white wine
Juice from ½ lemon

Cut the scrod into 4 equal portions, 8 ounces each. Finely chop the peppers and onion. Sauté the chopped vegetables in some oil with salt, pepper and garlic. When tender, place the pepper-onion mixture in a bowl. Add the butter, Tabasco sauce, Worcestershire sauce, gin and anisette. Mix well. Add the crushed crackers, mixing well.

Preheat oven to 400 degrees.

In a large ovenproof frying pan, cook the scrod in a little oil with the wine and lemon juice. When the fish begins to flake when touched with a fork, add the Ritz cracker crumb topping. Finish cooking the fish in the 400-degree oven. It is done when the topping begins to turn brown, approximately 30 minutes.

Recommended wine: *Ceretto Arneis*

If you're a restaurant with 'Lobstermania' in your name,
you probably know a thing or two about delicious lobster... enjoy!

DRESSING FOR STUFFED LOBSTER

(10 servings)

1 pound crushed Ritz crackers
1 cup bread crumbs
Pinch of garlic powder
Pinch of onion powder
Pinch of white pepper
¼ cup parsley flakes
2 tablespoons Worcestershire sauce
4 tablespoons white wine
1 stick margarine, melted
½ pound tiny shrimp
½ pound baby scallops
10 lobsters, approximately 1 and ¼ pounds each, split open

Preheat oven to 400 degrees.

In a large bowl, mix all the dry ingredients together. Add the liquid ingredients and mix well.
Add the shrimp and scallops. Mix well. Form this mixture into 10 equal size balls. Place the balls
on a baking sheet and bake in the 400-degree oven for 6 to 8 minutes. Place a precooked ball into
the cavity of a split lobster. Bake the lobsters in the 400-degree oven for approximately 12 to 15
minutes. Serve immediately.

Chef: Watthanarom Premwat

Owner: Haruki Kibe

Cuisine: Japanese

Specialty: Sushi

Price range: Appetizers,
$5 to $15

Entrees,
$12 to $30

Hours: Open seven days a week

Monday through Thursday,
noon to 10 pm

Friday and Saturday,
noon to 11 pm

Sunday,
4:30 to 10 pm

I love any recipe where I get to use sake! Not to mention the fact that Haruki East is one of southern New England's best Japanese restaurants.

SEAFOOD YAKISOBA
(3 servings)

1 tablespoon oyster sauce
1 tablespoon soy sauce
1 tablespoon mirin
1 tablespoon sake
2 teaspoons sugar
1 teaspoon chili flakes
1 tablespoon extra virgin olive oil
2 tablespoons sesame oil
¾ pound large shrimp, shelled and deveined
¾ pound jumbo scallops
Salt and pepper, to taste
1 large garlic clove, finely minced
1 red bell pepper, cut into thin julienne slices
4 ounces (½ cup) green beans, cut into 1-inch pieces
2 ounces (¼ cup) shiitake mushrooms, stems removed, sliced ½-inch thick
½ pound nappa cabbage, cut into 2-inch pieces
½ cup water
3 packages soba noodles
Pickled ginger, as needed

In a bowl, combine the oyster sauce, soy sauce, mirin, sake, sugar and chili flakes.

In a large nonstick skillet, heat the olive oil and sesame oil. Add the shrimp and scallops. Season with salt and pepper. Add the garlic, peppers, green beans, mushrooms, and cook for about 30 seconds. Add the cabbage, and cook for another 30 seconds. Add the water and noodles. Cook for about 1 minute, then add the oyster sauce mixture. Cook until the liquid is nearly evaporated, about 3 minutes. Transfer to a bowl, and serve immediately with pickled ginger.

Recommended wine: *Eroica Riesling*

One of our favorite things to do is to sit at the raw bar with a glass of perfectly chilled white wine. It just doesn't get much better than that.

GRILLED PORTUGUESE LITTLENECKS

(1 serving)

8 littleneck clams, scrubbed well
2 tablespoons butter
1 tablespoon chopped garlic
¼ pound chorizo, skin removed and diced
¼ cup white wine
1 tablespoon chopped scallions
¼ cup diced seedless tomatoes
1 teaspoon chopped parsley
1 lemon wedge

Place the clams on a hot grill and begin cooking. In a 9-inch sauté pan on the grill, combine the butter, garlic, chorizo, wine, scallions and tomatoes. When the clams open their shells, place them in the sauté pan and toss to coat well. Allow to simmer for 3 minutes. Arrange the clams in a soup bowl. Pour the remaining mixture over the clams. Sprinkle the clams with parsley. Garnish with the lemon wedge.

Chef's note: Do not overcook the clams. They should be removed from the grill as soon as the shells open fully. This recipe can also be served over rice or pasta. It is also easy to double this recipe.

Recommended wine: *Chateau Ste Michelle Horse Heaven Sauvignon Blanc*

HORTON'S SEAFOOD

809 Broadway
East Providence, RI
401-434-3116

Chefs: Jonathan Couto
and Heather Coogan

Owners: Heather and
Brian Coogan

Cuisine: Seafood

Specialty: Fried clams

Signature dish: Fish and chips

Price range: Appetizers,
$1.25 to $8

Entrees,
$9 to $22

Hours: Wednesday, Thursday
and Saturday,
11 am to 8 pm

Friday,
10 am to 9 pm

This is the only recipe we could pry out of the vault at Horton's Seafood, which is understandable since they are quite possibly the best seafood shack in Rhode Island, and only minutes from downtown Providence.

CREAMY COLE SLAW
(12 servings)

32 ounces (4 cups) Hellmann's mayonnaise
10 ounces (1 and ¼ cups) granulated sugar
7 shakes of malt vinegar
5 pounds freshly shredded cabbage
1 carrot, shredded

In a very large bowl, mix together the mayonnaise, sugar and vinegar until smooth — it should have the consistency of pudding. Add the shredded cabbage and carrot. Mix well. Refrigerate until it is time to serve.

Chef's note: This is the cole slaw we serve with all our seafood dishes. It's especially good with fish and chips.

This intimate, popular Italian restaurant is known for classic dishes like this. Mangia bene!

IL FORNELLO

16 Josephine Street
North Providence, RI
401-722-5599
www.ilfornellori.com

SCROD CIOPPINO
(4 servings)

4 cod fillets, 6 to 8 ounces each
2 teaspoons extra virgin olive oil
1 medium onion, sliced
2 garlic cloves, minced or chopped
1 pound mussels
12 littleneck clams, still in the shell
1 cup white wine
1 pound large shrimp (8 to 12 per pound), shelled and deveined
Tomato sauce, as needed
Salt and pepper, to taste
Chopped parsley, as needed
4 fresh basil leaves

Bake the cod in a preheated 350-degree oven to start the cooking process.

In a large stock pot, heat the olive oil. Add the onions and garlic; sauté until golden brown. Add the mussels, clams and wine. Cover and simmer until the shellfish have opened. Add the shrimp and tomato sauce, enough to cover everything in the pot. Simmer until the shrimp are cooked, 5 to 7 minutes. Season with salt and pepper.

Place the scrod on a serving platter or on individual plates. Spoon the seafood and sauce over the scrod. Garnish with chopped parsley and fresh basil.

Recommended wine: *Mastroberardino Greco di Tufo*

Chef:	Phil Nasisi
Owners:	Tony Lanni and Phil Nasisi
Cuisine:	Authentic Italian
Price range:	Appetizers, $8 to $12
	Entrees, $15 to $20
Hours:	Monday through Saturday, 5 to 10 pm
	Sunday, open for private functions only

JOE MARZILLI'S OLD CANTEEN

120 Atwells Avenue
Providence, RI
401-751-5544

Chefs: Sal Marzilli and
Phil Manning

Owner: Emma Marzilli

Cuisine: Classic Italian
and American

Specialty: Veal and fresh
local seafood

Signature dish: Haddock
Sicilian-Style

Price range: Appetizers,
$9 to $15

Entrees,
$15 to $22

Hours: Wednesday
through Monday,
11:30 am to 10 pm

Businessman luncheon served daily,
11:30 am to 3 pm

This recipe is given in memory of one of the great Rhode Island restaurateurs, Joe Marzilli, by my good friend, his son, Sal. Thanks for the memories, Mr. M!

ESCAROLE AND BEAN SOUP
(10 to 12 servings)

5 tablespoons extra virgin olive oil, divided
1 large onion, diced
36 ounces (4 and ½ cups) low-sodium chicken stock
Salt and freshly ground black pepper, to taste
¼ teaspoon garlic powder
2 (8-ounce) cans Great Northern beans, drained
1 large head escarole, washed and finely chopped
1 pinch red pepper flakes
1 cup freshly grated Pecorino Romano cheese

In a large stock pot, heat 3 tablespoons of olive oil. Add the diced onion, and sauté for 5 minutes or until translucent. Add the chicken stock. Bring to a boil, then simmer for 15 minutes. Taste and season with salt, pepper and garlic powder. Bring to a boil again, add the beans, and reduce to a simmer.

About 5 minutes before serving, add the chopped escarole, red pepper flakes, and remaining olive oil. Serve in heated bowls along with the freshly grated cheese.

I expect nothing less than the extraordinary from Julian and his unique Broadway eatery.

COD, BLACK BEAN AND VIDALIA ONION FRITTERS
(12 servings)

1 pound fritter mix (available in seafood markets)
1 cup chopped cod
¼ cup blanched black beans
¼ cup minced Vidalia onions
1 cup ice cold water
Salt and pepper, to taste

Aioli:
2 egg yolks
2 garlic cloves
1 roasted red pepper, skin and seeds removed
4 large basil leaves
Juice from 2 large lemons
¾ cup extra virgin olive oil

In a large mixing bowl, combine the fritter mix with the chopped cod, black beans, onions, water, salt and pepper. Do not over mix. Set aside for 10 minutes. Using an ice cream scoop as a measure, deep fry the balls of batter in oil heated to 350 degrees until the fritters are golden, 4 to 5 minutes. Using a large slotted metal spoon, remove the fritters from the oil and allow to drain on a paper towel.

In a food processor, combine all the aioli ingredients except for the olive oil. Blend well. With the processor running, slowly drizzle in the oil until the aioli has the consistency of mayonnaise. Serve the aioli on the side with the fritters.

KABOB AND CURRY

261 Thayer Street
Providence, RI
401-273-8844
www.kabobandcurry.com

Chef/owner:	Sanjiv Dhar
Cuisine:	Indian
Specialty:	Authentic Indian cuisine for the American palate
Signature dish:	Chicken Tikka Masala
Price range:	Appetizers, $3 to $9
	Entrees, $9.50 to $18
Hours:	Open seven days a week
	Monday through Thursday, 11 am to 10:30 pm
	Friday and Saturday, 11 am to 11 pm
	Sunday, 11:30 am to 10 pm

The incredible aroma of the spices will fill your kitchen...

CHICKEN XACUTI

(2 servings)

1 pound chicken tenders
⅓ cup vegetable oil
1 cup grated coconut
2 cinnamon sticks, 1-inch long
6 cloves
2 dry red chili peppers
½ teaspoon turmeric powder
2 tablespoons poppy seeds
1 teaspoon carom seeds
1 teaspoon cumin seeds
1 teaspoon black peppercorns

1 teaspoon fennel seeds
2 star anise
1 teaspoon coriander seeds
4 garlic cloves
2 medium-size onions, peeled and finely chopped
2 cups water
Salt, to taste
1 tablespoon tamarind paste
¼ teaspoon grated nutmeg

Chef's note: Many of these ingredients are available in Indian food markets and spice shops.

Preheat oven to 350 degrees.

Rinse the chicken, and cut each tender into 3 pieces. In a sauté pan, heat a little oil and slightly brown the grated coconut. Set aside. Dry roast all the spices in an ovenproof dish in the 350-degree oven just until you can detect a pleasant aroma. Grind the roasted spices into a paste together with the coconut and garlic to make a masala.

Heat the remaining oil in a heavy-bottomed pan. Sauté the finely chopped onions until brown. Add the masala paste, and sauté until the oil separates. Add the chicken pieces, and sauté for 2 to 3 minutes, constantly stirring. Add the water, and bring to a boil. Season with salt, tamarind paste and grated nutmeg. Simmer for 5 minutes or until the sauce thickens. Serve immediately. This is excellent with steamed basmati rice.

Recommended wine: *Trimbach Gewurtztraminer*

Sanjiv Dhar

o much so you might want to take up the sitar.

LA PRIMA CAFFE

205 Broadway
Providence, RI
401-331-6507
www.laprimacaffe.com

Chef/Owner: Philip R. McKendall

Cuisine: Regional/Continental

Specialty: Authentic Italian dishes

Signature dish: Tortellini
di Filippo

Price range: Appetizers,
$8 to $11

Entrees,
$15 to $25

Hours: Monday through Friday,
7 am to 3 pm

Saturday,
8 am to 2 pm

Dinner served
Thursday through Saturday,
5:30 to 10 pm

This bustling little Italian kitchen by day and great jazz caffe at night boasts big-time Italian food, courtesy of chef/owner Phil.

PROSCIUTTO E PISELLI GARGANELLI
(PASTA WITH PROSCIUTTO AND PEAS)

(4 servings)

1 pound fresh garganelli (from Venda Ravioli) or dry (from Famoso)*
5 tablespoons salted butter
⅛ pound San Daniele or Parma prosciutto, diced
½ cup peas, fresh or frozen
1 and ½ cups heavy cream
½ cup grated Parmigian cheese
Kosher salt, to taste
Garlic powder, to taste

*Garganelli are grooved tubes of pasta made from dough that contains cheese. If you can't find garganelli, you could use tortellini instead.

In a large pot of boiling water, cook the pasta until al dente (fresh pasta will cook in 2 to 5 minutes, dry pasta in 7 to 11 minutes). Drain and set aside to cool.

In a large deep sauté or saucepan over medium to high heat, melt the butter. Add the prosciutto. Stir and cook for 2 minutes. Add the peas and heavy cream. When cream starts to boil, add half of the cheese and stir. When the sauce starts to thicken, add the cooked pasta and remaining cheese. Add 3 pinches of kosher salt and 2 pinches of garlic powder, more or less to taste. Fold mixture together. Transfer mixture to a large warm pasta bowl for serving at the table.

Recommended wine: *Planeta La Segreta Bianco*

Cooking in the designer kitchens at S & W Television and Appliance showroom in East Providence with...

Chef Sal Marzilli, Joe Marzilli's Old Canteen

Chef Phyllis Arffa, Blaze

Susan DeAngelus and Chef Bill Smith,
Twin Oaks

Chef Emily Spinazola,
Providence Oyster Bar and Providence Prime

Chef John Richardson, Pot au Feu

Chef John Granata, Camille's

LJ'S BBQ

727 East Avenue
Pawtucket, RI
401-305-5255
www.LJSBBQ.com

Chef: Bernard Watson

Owners: Bernard and
                  Linda Watson

Cuisine: Southern-inspired
   home-style cooking and BBQ

Specialty: Smoked Prime Rib
          (weekends only) and
             Pulled Pork BBQ

Signature dish: Pulled Pork Pizza

Price range: Appetizers,
             $2.25 to $10.25

                     Entrees,
             $8.25 to $23.25

Hours: Open seven days a week,
        11:30 am to closing,
    serving lunch and dinner,
       and serving brunch on
         Saturday and Sunday,
           10 am to 2 pm.

I'm telling you, this rub would make furniture taste fabulous!

PORK RIB RUB

4 tablespoons light brown sugar, packed
3 tablespoons onion powder
3 tablespoons garlic powder
2 tablespoons dry mustard
3 tablespoons paprika
1 tablespoon Bell's Seasoning
2 tablespoons dried thyme
2 tablespoons chili powder
1 tablespoon black pepper
1 tablespoon salt

Mix all the above ingredients together. Store in a resealable plastic bag. When ready to use, sprinkle 2 tablespoons of the mixture on a slab of pork ribs. Massage the mixture into the meat. Wrap the ribs in plastic wrap and refrigerate for 24 hours to allow the rub to tenderize and season the meat. Proceed with the cooking of the spare ribs as usual.

Bernie Watson

Eat It 'n Beat It!

Chef: Brian Ruffner

Owner: Mario Macera

Cuisine: Italian

Specialty: Pasta, veal, chicken and seafood

Signature dish: Pasta L'Osteria

Price range: Appetizers, $9 to $13

Entrees, $14 to $23

Hours: Tuesday through Saturday, 4:30 pm to closing

This restaurant is truly an authentic Italian oasis in Cranston's delicious little Knightsville section where great Italian food is a given.

CHICKEN UNDER A BRICK
(4 servings)

1 cup oil
2 tablespoons sugar
1 tablespoon basil
1 tablespoon Cajun seasoning
Salt and pepper, to taste
4 (8-ounce) boneless chicken breasts cut horizontally to make 8 scaloppine-style filets
2 tablespoons pure olive oil
1 and ½ tablespoons chopped garlic
2 teaspoons crushed chili flakes
4 ounces (½ cup) rehydrated porcini mushrooms,
    or 6 ounces (¾ cup) fresh portabello mushrooms, diced
3 cups drained white northern or cannellini beans
1 cup chicken stock
2 ounces (¼ cup) sun-dried tomatoes, cut into thin julienne strips
4 tablespoons unsalted butter
4 tablespoons chopped Italian parsley

Combine the oil, sugar, basil, Cajun seasoning, salt and pepper. Marinate the chicken in this mixture for 1 hour in the refrigerator. Preheat a grill for approximately 15 minutes.

In a sauté pan, heat the olive oil. Sauté the garlic in the oil until golden. Add the chili flakes, mushrooms and beans. Add the chicken stock. Bring to a boil, and reduce to a simmer. Add the sun-dried tomatoes, butter, and 1 tablespoon of parsley to the mixture.

Wrap a brick (the type used to build fireplaces) in aluminum foil. Place the brick on top of the chicken on the grill. Cook the chicken on the grill, being careful to avoid flames, for 3 to 4 minutes on each side or until done, depending on the thickness of the chicken.

Heap approximately ¾ cup of the mushroom-bean mixture in the center of a warm dinner plate. Place 2 pieces of chicken on top of the ragout. Sprinkle each plate with remaining parsley, and drizzle with a little extra virgin olive oil. Serve immediately with a salad or vegetable side dish.

Recommended wine: *Planeta Syrah*

This signature recipe is from one of my favorite southern New England restaurants and named in honor of one of my favorite restaurateurs, Luciano Canova.

VEAL CHOPS ALLA LUCIANO

(2 servings)

12-ounce bone-in Provimi veal chop, one per person
⅓ cup lobster meat, per chop
2 ounces imported buffalo mozzarella, per chop
1 ounce imported prosciutto, per chop
Flour, as needed
2 eggs, beaten
Bread crumbs, as needed
Olive oil, as needed

Mushroom Marsala Sauce:
2 tablespoons butter, divided
1 shallot, sliced
1 cup sliced mushrooms, domestic and porcini
½ cup Marsala wine
½ cup heavy cream
¼ cup chopped parsley
Parmigiano-reggiano cheese, as needed

Preheat oven to 350 degrees.

Butterfly each veal chop; that is, using a small sharp knife, cut a deep pocket into the chop and spread it open. Pound the meat with a meat mallet to tenderize it. Into the pocket, place the lobster meat, mozzarella and prosciutto. Close the pocket to reform the veal chop. Dredge the chop in flour, then in the beaten egg, then in the bread crumbs. In a large ovenproof frying pan, heat enough olive oil to cover the bottom of the pan. Pan-sear the veal chop in the oil until golden brown on both sides. Place the veal chops in the 350-degree oven and bake for 15 minutes.

During that time, make the sauce. In a large frying pan, melt 1 tablespoon of butter. Sauté the shallots and mushrooms in the melted butter. Add the wine and heavy cream. Simmer for 10 minutes. Continue to simmer until the liquid is reduced to half. Finish the sauce by swirling in the remaining butter and parsley.

Remove the veal chops from the oven, and place them on warm dinner plates. Pour some sauce over each chop. Sprinkle each chop with some Parmigiano-reggiano cheese. Serve immediately.

Recommended wine: *Sandrone Barbera d'Alba*

MAIN STREET COFFEE

137 Main Street
East Greenwich, RI
401-885-8787

Come on! It's time you buy an espresso machine, and you know it!
By the way, don't hesitate to add your favorite spirit to this fabulous drink.

BARISTA'S CHOICE RICH CARAMEL MOCHA

(I serving)

¾ ounce Guittard Rich & Creamy Caramel Syrup*
¾ ounce Guittard Sweet Ground Chocolate Syrup*
2 shots freshly ground espresso coffee
I cup cold milk
Freshly whipped cream, as needed
Chocolate sprinkles, as needed

In a 16-ounce glass mug, combine the caramel syrup, chocolate syrup and espresso. Steam the milk in a steaming pitcher. Pour the steamed milk into the glass mug. Mix well. Top with whipped cream and chocolate sprinkles.

* Ghirardelli syrups may be used in place of Guittard.

Barista: Mike Monti

Owners: Steve and Jean
                          Cinquegrana

Cuisine: Light lunch
                          and appetizers

Signature dish: Chicken Pesto
                          Parmigiano Panini

Price range: $6 to $8

Hours: Open seven days a week

Monday through Thursday
and Sunday,
6 am to 10 pm

Friday and Saturday,
6 am to I am

A recipe like this is truly one of the great things about being a Rhode Islander... this, and vanity plates, of course.

FISHERMAN-STYLE BAKED STUFFED LOBSTER
(1 serving)

1 lobster, 2 pounds
1 extra large shrimp, peeled and deveined
3 large scallops, trimmed
½ cup crushed Ritz crackers
3 tablespoons butter, melted
2 tablespoons sherry
Salt, as needed
Additional melted butter, for dipping

Split the lobster lengthwise, and place the split lobster in a large shallow baking pan. Clean out the cavity of the lobster. Break off the legs and claws and place them in boiling water for 3 minutes. Allow the legs and claws to cool, then crack them open and remove the meat. Pack the lobster meat, shrimp and scallops into the cavity.

Preheat oven to 425 degrees.

In a bowl, combine the crushed Ritz crackers with most of the butter and sherry. Cover the stuffed lobster cavity with the cracker mixture. Drizzle the remaining butter on top. Pour enough water to cover the bottom of the pan. Add a pinch of salt to the water. Cover the entire pan with aluminum foil. Place the pan in the 425-degree oven and bake for 15 minutes. Remove the foil and bake for another 5 minutes. Serve with additional melted butter.

Recommended wine: *Rombauer Chardonnay*

MARIO'S RISTO BAR

20 Haven Avenue
Cranston, RI
401-942-1009

Chef: Mario Santilli

Owners: Mario and Carol Santilli

Cuisine: Italian

Specialty: Steaks and seafood

Signature dish: Veal Mario

Price range: Appetizers,
$9 and up

Entrees,
$15 and up

Hours: Tuesday through Thursday,
11:30 am to 9 pm

Friday,
11:30 am to 10 pm

Saturday,
5 to 10 pm

Open on Sunday only
for private parties

My friend, Chef Mario, has created a seafood explosion of flavor. Bring your appetite!

SCROD ALLA PESCATORA OVER LINGUINE
(2 servings)

½ cup olive oil
5 garlic cloves
1 pound fresh scrod
Salt and pepper, to taste
Flour, as needed
8 whole littleneck clams
1 pint (2 cups) chopped littleneck clams
1 pound calamari, cut into rings
½ cup red wine
½ cup clam juice
4 cups whole peeled tomatoes, crushed by hand
4 sprigs fresh basil, torn into pieces
4 sprigs fresh parsley, chopped
½ pound linguine

In a large sauté pan, heat the olive oil. Add the garlic, and cook until golden brown. Season the scrod with the salt and pepper, then dust lightly with the flour. Place the scrod in the pan along with the whole littleneck clams, chopped littleneck clams and calamari. Pan-sear the scrod on both sides until golden brown. Remove the scrod and whole littleneck clams from the pan and set aside; keep warm. To the pan, add the red wine and allow it to evaporate over medium-high heat. Add the clam juice, crushed tomatoes and fresh herbs. Cover and simmer for 5 to 7 minutes on low heat.

In a pot of boiling salted water, cook the linguine until al dente. Drain well. Place the cooked pasta in a large warm bowl, and toss with half of the sauce. Pour the pasta onto a large warm serving platter. Top with the cooked scrod and whole littleneck clams. Pour the remaining sauce over the entire dish. Garnish with fresh basil, if desired.

Recommended wine: *Pieropan Soave Classico*

In the kitchen with...

Chef Sai Viswanath,
DeWolf Tavern

Chef Nick Iannuccilli, Rodizio,
and Gian Carlo Iannuccilli,
Gian Carlo's Ristorante

Chef Phil McKendall, La Prima Caffe

Chef Tammie Watson, Bay Leaves

MEDITERRANEO

134 Atwells Avenue
Providence, RI
401-331-7760
www.mediterraneocaffe.com

Chefs: Gianfranco Campanella,
Michele Calise and
Giulio Medizza

Owners: Gianfranco Marrocco,
Gaetano Marrocco and
Dr. Fabio Potenti

Cuisine: Traditional and
contemporary Italian

Price range: Appetizers,
$7.95 to $12.95

Entrees,
$15.95 to $34.95

Hours: Open seven days a week

Lunch on
Monday through Friday
starting at 11:30 am

Dinner every night
from 4:30 pm until closing

Warning: This dish may be addictive!

SAFFRON RISOTTO

(4 servings)

2 tablespoons extra virgin olive oil
2 shallots, peeled and finely diced
2 garlic cloves, finely chopped
1 cup white wine
12 ounces (1 and ½ cups) arborio rice
10 cups chicken broth or water
2 pinches saffron
Salt and pepper, to taste
½ cup heavy cream
2 tablespoons butter

In a medium-size sauté pan over medium heat, combine the olive oil, shallots and garlic. Sauté until translucent. Deglaze the pan with white wine. Add the rice, and sauté until it begins to turn translucent, approximately 1 minute.

Add the chicken broth in small amounts until the rice is covered. Add the saffron, salt and pepper. When the rice is half cooked, add the cream and additional chicken broth, if necessary. Once the rice is completely cooked, add the butter, swirling it into the rice. Serve immediately.

Fabio, Gian and Nino

You'll be craving more!

MILL'S TAVERN

101 North Main Street
Providence, RI
401-272-3331

Chef: Christian Robert Pieper

Owner: Jaime D'Oliveira

Cuisine: Contemporary American

Specialty: Wood-fire cooking

Signature dish: Eight-Hour Ruby
Port Braised Short Ribs

Price range: Appetizers,
$7 to $14

Entrees,
$18 to $40

Hours: Open seven days a week

Monday to Thursday,
5 to 10 pm

Friday and Saturday,
5 to 11 pm

Sunday,
4 to 9 pm

Delicate and delicious. I love recipes that pay attention to those little things that make a dish great... case in point, this superb vinaigrette.

PAN-SEARED RHODE ISLAND SCALLOPS WITH BEET VINAIGRETTE

(4 servings)

1 large beet, roasted in 375-degree oven for 2 hours and peeled
2 tablespoons honey
2 tablespoons whole-grain mustard
2 tablespoons chopped shallots
4 tablespoons sherry vinegar
Salt and pepper, to taste
1 and ½ cups canola oil
4 tablespoons canola oil, for frying
12 extra-large local scallops (U-10 are recommended)
2 tablespoons butter
Garnish: Deep-fried wonton skins (optional)

To make the vinaigrette, combine the roasted beet, honey, mustard, shallots, sherry vinegar, salt and pepper. Puree in a blender. Once smooth, add the oil slowly. Check the taste for additional seasoning.

In a large sauté pan, heat the 4 tablespoons of oil until the pan is smoking. Season the scallops lightly with salt and pepper. Sear the scallops in the hot sauté pan for 3 to 4 minutes, or until the scallops are caramelized. Turn the scallops over. Add the butter, lower the heat, and cook until medium rare.

Place 3 scallops on each serving plate, caramelized side up. Drizzle with vinaigrette. Garnish with deep-fried wonton skins, if desired.

Chef's note: At Mill's Tavern, we serve this with Pancetta and Blue Crab Hash.

Recommended wine: *Chateau Ste Michelle Pinot Gris*

There are a lot of incredible scallop recipes in this book. But, this is the only one that I'll enjoy with three packs of oyster crackers! Yeah... "chow–duh."

SCALLOP CHOWDER

(Makes 1 gallon, 10 servings)

½ pound butter (2 sticks)
1 Spanish onion, diced
1 and ½ cups all-purpose flour
12 cups hot water
2 cups white wine
¼ cup clam base
½ fresh chopped parsley
¼ cup chopped fresh dill, or less to taste
4 bay leaves
2 cups half-and-half, more or less as needed
2 pounds scallops
1 cup corn niblets

In a heavy-bottomed large stockpot, melt butter over medium heat. Add the onions and sauté until translucent. Add the flour to make a roux; cook for 5 minutes over low flame, stirring constantly. Slowly incorporate the hot water while stirring with a whisk to avoid lumps. Add the wine, clam base and seasonings. Simmer for 30 to 45 minutes over low heat.

Whisk in a desired amount of half-and-half. Slowly poach a desired amount of scallops in the chowder until the scallops are firm. Add the corn niblets. Remove the bay leaves from the chowder. Serve immediately.

MURPHY'S DELI

100 Fountain Street
Providence, RI
401-621-8467
and 401-421-1188

Chef: Julie Ferrazzano-Mazza

Owner: Ruth Ferrazzano

Cuisine: Home-style American favorites, New York deli, pub food

Specialty: Grilled Reuben Sandwiches

Signature dish: Shepherd's Pie and other specials

Price range: Appetizers, $5.50 to $9

Entrees, $4.25 to $16

Hours: Monday through Thursday, 11 am to midnight

Friday and Saturday, 11 am to 1 am

Sunday, noon to midnight

One of my all time favorite Providence hangouts. This recipe calls for 2 pints of Guinness. I say add another! Put two in the pan and one in you. Now you're livin'!

JULIE'S GUINNESS BEEF STEW
(6 servings)

2 cups all-purpose flour
Kosher salt, to taste
Ground black pepper, to taste
Granulated garlic, to taste
3 pounds Black Angus top round, cut into 2-inch cubes
¼ cup extra virgin olive oil
4 tablespoons (½ stick) salted butter
2 medium-size Vidalia onions, chopped fine
1 cup minced garlic in oil

1 cup finely chopped scallions
4 sprigs fresh thyme
2 tablespoons tomato paste
2 pints (4 cups) Guinness Stout Beer
8 cups beef stock, store-bought or homemade
4 cups pearl onions, frozen
4 celery stalks, cut into ½-inch pieces
4 medium-size carrots, cut into ½-inch pieces
2 pounds red bliss potatoes, quartered

In a large deep bowl, combine the flour, kosher salt, black pepper, and granulated garlic. Add the cubed beef to the bowl, and dredge the beef until it is all thoroughly covered with the flour. In a large pan over medium-low heat, combine the olive oil and butter. Once the butter has melted, begin to add the pieces of dredged beef in batches. Do not over load the pan. As the beef becomes golden brown on both sides, remove these pieces and continue to add all pieces until all the beef has been browned and removed to a separate plate. Use a wooden spoon to loosen any beef bits that are attached to the bottom of the pan, and then add the chopped onions, minced garlic, scallions, thyme (removed from the sprig), more salt, pepper and granulated garlic. Stir constantly.

Once the onions appear "glazed" in color, add the tomato paste and mix well, then add the beer. When the beer begins to simmer, add the browned beef, beef stock, pearl onions, celery, carrots, potatoes, more salt, pepper and granulated garlic. Let the stew simmer for at least 2 hours.

Chef's note: The longer it simmers on low, the thicker and more tastier it is. Remember, the salt, pepper and granulated garlic are "to taste." You can always add it in, but you can't take it out! We recommend going very easy on the seasoning, and add more if needed during the simmering process. This stew is perfect with buttermilk biscuits.

Recommended wine: *Bookwalter Lot 21 Proprietary Blend*

Now, get your head out of the sand (sorry, I couldn't resist) and understand that you're bordering on true "chefhood" when you prepare this. And the cherry demi is out of this world!

NAPA VALLEY GRILLE

111 Providence Place
Providence, RI
401-270-6272
www.napavalleygrille.com

CHERRY DEMI OSTRICH

(2 servings)

Cherry Demi Sauce:
2 tablespoons vegetable oil
½ large carrot, chopped
1 large onion, chopped
2 garlic cloves
1 pound dry cherries
1 and ½ cups port wine
4 thyme sprigs
2 rosemary sprigs
2 quarts veal stock
Kosher salt and black pepper, as needed

1 pound ostrich fan thigh filet
Maple syrup, as needed
Napa Spice, to taste

In a large frying pan in hot oil, sauté the carrots, onions, garlic and half the cherries, being careful not to burn the cherries. Deglaze the pan with the wine, and continue to cook until the sauce is reduced by half. Add the thyme, rosemary and veal stock. Simmer for 35 minutes on medium heat. Strain, then add the remaining cherries. Season with salt and pepper.

Marinate the ostrich in maple syrup and Napa Spice (which may be purchased at Napa Valley Grille). Grill the ostrich until medium rare. Serve immediately, drizzled with the cherry demi sauce.

Recommended wine: *DeLisio Grenache*

Chef:	Jeffrey Carroll
Cuisine:	Wine Country
Specialty:	Seasonal and rustic dishes
Price range:	Appetizers, $7 to $15
	Entrees, $17 to $34
Hours:	Open seven days a week
	Monday through Saturday, 11:30 am to closing
	Sunday, 11:30 am to 9 pm

NEWPORT BLUES CAFE

286 Thames Street
Newport, RI
401-841-5510
www.newportblues.com

Chef: William James

Cuisine: Seafood/Continental

Signature dish: Blues Café-Style Crab Cakes

Price range: Appetizers, $7 to $12

Entrees, $13 to $21

Hours: Open seven days a week, 6 pm to 1 am

Rumor has it that if you put this recipe to your ear, you'll hear B.B. King!

CLASSIC CRAB CAKES
(8 servings)

1 pound jumbo lump crab meat
1 cup mayonnaise
1 cup breadcrumbs, or more if needed
4 eggs
1 bunch scallions, chopped
1 red bell pepper, chopped fine
1 green bell pepper, chopped fine
Crushed red pepper flakes, to taste
¼ teaspoon Old Bay Seasoning
2 tablespoons Worcestershire sauce
2 tablespoons lemon juice
Oil, for frying

In a large bowl, combine all the ingredients except the oil. Mix well. Let sit for a short time. If too watery, add more breadcrumbs. Form patties that weight about 2 ounces each. In a large sauté pan, fry the patties in a little bit of oil until golden brown on both sides. Serve immediately.

Recommended wine: *Cloudy Bay Sauvignon Blanc*

Don't be fooled by the name of this recipe. There's actually an incredible array of flavorful ingredients. I'm trying to figure out how a speck of "speck"' got top billing.

OCTAGON

At the Mystic Marriott
Hotel & Spa
625 North Road
Groton, CT
860-326-0360
waterfordgrouprestaurants
.com/octagon/

NATIVE SEA SCALLOPS WITH SPECK

(1 serving)

3 ounces (almost ½ cup) risotto, cooked al dente
2 cloves roasted garlic
4 tablespoons olive oil, divided
½ pound fresh sea scallops, cleaned and dried
Salt and pepper, to taste
Nappa cabbage, thinly sliced, as needed
1 ounce speck (a cured ham similar to prosciutto)
6 tablespoons Chardonnay wine
2 tablespoons Chardonnay vinegar or lemon juice
2 tablespoons butter
Baby green beans, trimmed and blanched, as needed
Fresh herbs, as needed, for garnish

Prepare the risotto ahead of time according to package directions. Add the roasted garlic and 2 tablespoons of olive oil to the risotto.

Season the scallops lightly with the salt and pepper. In a 10-inch sauté pan, heat the remaining olive oil and sear the scallops 1 to 2 minutes, or until they are golden brown. Flip the scallops over and cook another 1 to 2 minutes. Remove the cooked scallops from the pan and set aside. Into the pan, add the cabbage and speck. Cook for about 1 minute, then remove from the pan and set aside. Add the wine and vinegar to the pan, and reduce by one-half over medium-high heat. Whip in the butter. Pour this sauce onto a warm dinner plate.

Add the risotto, cabbage and speck back into the pan over medium-high heat. When heated through, pour this mixture on top of the sauce in the center of the dinner plate.

In a clean sauté pan, warm the green beans and scallops. Arrange the green beans and scallops over the risotto mixture. Garnish with fresh herbs. Serve immediately. This recipe can easily be doubled.

Recommended wine: *DeForville Chardonnary Piemonte*

Chef:	Steve Rosen
Owner:	Waterford Group Restaurants
Cuisine:	Creative American
Specialty:	Composed plates
Signature dish:	Chili-Rubbed Certified Angus Beef Bone-in Ribeye (24 ounces)
Price range:	Appetizers, $1.75 (from the raw bar) to $16
	Entrees, $19 to $39
Hours:	Open seven days a week for dinner, 5:30 to 10 pm

PAL'S RESTAURANT

43 Division Street
East Greenwich, RI
401-884-9701
www.trcri.com

Chef: Ronny Ware

Cuisine: Italian

Specialty: Veal, beef, and seafood

Signature dish: Veal Sinatra

Price range: Appetizers, $6 to $16

Entrees, $8 to $22

Hours: Open seven days a week

Monday, from 4 pm

Tuesday through Saturday, from 11:30 am

Sunday, from 12:30 pm

This delicious recipe comes with a great story from Pal's owner Ronny Ware. He first enjoyed this dish which was created by 'ol Blue Eyes himself (talk about a special order!) at Paesano's in Fort Lauderdale, Florida. Ronny dined there and loved the dish so much he asked Paesano's for permission to put it on his menu. Now you can eat like Frank in your home or at Pal's in East Greenwich... dooby dooby doo!

VEAL SINATRA

(1 serving)

1 tablespoon olive oil
Flour, as needed
4 (1-ounce) veal medallions
Marsala wine, as needed
Salt and pepper, to taste
Garlic powder, to taste
4 thin slices prosciutto
2 ounces sliced mushrooms
2 ounces washed spinach
¼ cup grated Romano cheese
½ cup marinara sauce
1 tablespoon butter
1 tablespoon heavy cream
Mozzarella cheese, as needed

Preheat oven to 400 degrees.

In an ovenproof sauté pan, heat the olive oil. Flour the veal medallions and place them in the sauté pan. Cook lightly on both sides. Add a splash of Marsala wine, and allow it to burn off. Season the veal with salt, pepper and garlic powder. Add the prosciutto to the sides of the sauté pan. Top the veal with the sliced mushrooms and spinach. Sprinkle the Romano cheese on top. Add the marinara sauce, butter and heavy cream to the sauté pan. Mix well and simmer on medium heat for 5 to 10 minutes.

Top with the mozzarella cheese. Place the sauté pan in a preheated 400-degree oven for 2 minutes. Serve immediately.

Recommended wine: *Carpineto Vino Nobile di Montepulciano*

Pane e Vino means bread and wine, two staples of Italian culture
that perfectly complement this wonderful Neapolitan dish.
(And gamberi sounds so much more romantic than shrimp!)

PANE E VINO

365 Atwells Avenue
Providence, RI
401-223-2230
www.panevino.net

RIGATONI GAMBERI
(RIGATONI WITH SHRIMP)

(2 servings)

8 ounces rigatoni pasta
4 tablespoons vegetable oil
2 garlic cloves, smashed
12 extra-large shrimp
8 asparagus tips
10 cherry tomatoes, cut in half
¼ cup white wine
Salt and pepper, to taste
Pinch of red pepper flakes
4 tablespoons extra virgin olive oil

Cook the pasta according to directions on the package.

While the pasta is cooking, in a large frying pan, combine the vegetable oil and garlic. Bring to medium-high heat, allowing the garlic to flavor the oil, about 2 minutes. Discard the garlic. Add the shrimp to the pan. Turn the shrimp to cook on both sides, about 2 to 3 minutes for each side. Add the asparagus tips and cherry tomatoes, tossing in the pan to coat well. When the asparagus begins to turn bright green and the tomato begins to soften, remove the pan from the heat and add the wine. Return the pan to the heat. Add the salt, pepper and red pepper flakes. Simmer 1 to 2 minutes.

Drain the pasta, and add the cooked pasta to the frying pan. Drizzle with the olive oil and serve immediately.

Recommended wine: *Attems Pinot Bianco*

Owner: Joseph DeQuattro

Cuisine: Italian

Specialty: Rustic Mediterraneo
                  atmosphere

Price range: Appetizers,
                      $8 to $12

                          Entrees,
                      $15 to $34

Hours: Open seven days a week

                          Sunday,
                  noon to 9 pm

          Monday through Thursday,
                  5 to 10 pm

              Friday and Saturday,
                  5 to 11 pm

393 Charles Street
Providence, RI
401-331-3000
www.pearlrestaurant.net

Chef: Joseph Zacovic

Owner: Joseph M. Aloisio

Cuisine: Contemporary
               American/Nuevo

Specialty: Fusion cooking

Signature dish: Caribbean-Style
                 Pork Chops

Price range: Appetizers,
               $8 to $12

               Entrees,
               $16 to $42

Hours: Tuesday, Wednesday,
           Thursday and Sunday,
               5 to 11 pm

               Friday and Saturday,
               5 pm to midnight

This mouthwatering creation comes from the place I truly believe is one of the most stylish dining spots in Southern New England. Visit Pearl and be wowed! It's like a little bit of Vegas in Rhode Island.

POLLO AL FORNO

(2 servings)

½ bunch fresh thyme
½ bunch fresh oregano
2 chicken breasts (skin on), 10 to 12 ounces each
2 ounces fresh baby spinach
4 ounces fresh mozzarella, cut into slices
3 ounces sweet fire-roasted red peppers (canned)
2 tablespoons oil
Salt and pepper, to taste
Flour, as needed
2 tablespoons butter
2 large shallots, sliced
¼ cup Marsala wine or cognac
1 cup cream

Pull the leaves from the thyme and oregano stems, and finely chop the leaves. Discard stems. Preheat oven to 325 degrees.

Cut a pocket into each chicken breast lengthwise. Stuff the pockets with the baby spinach, mozzarella, and red peppers (make sure the cheese is in the center). Heat an ovenproof frying pan over medium-high heat with the oil for 2 minutes. Season the skin side of the chicken with salt and pepper. Dredge the skin side of the chicken in the chopped herbs and flour. Place the stuffed, seasoned chicken breasts into the frying pan skin side down. When the skin is golden brown, turn the breasts over. Place the pan in the 325-degree oven for 10 minutes, or until the chicken is done.

In a separate pan over medium heat, melt the butter and add the shallots. Cook until the shallots are translucent. Move the pan away from the heat. Add the wine or cognac. Return the pan to the heat. Cook for 30 seconds. Add the cream. Season to taste with salt and pepper. Remove the chicken breasts from the oven. Drizzle the sauce over the chicken breasts and serve immediately.

Recommended wine: *Monte Antico Rosso Toscana*

Deli by day... bustling, vibrant trattoria at night.
Pinelli's made its mark long ago as one of Rhode Island's most popular
B.Y.O.B restaurants with delicious and abundant Italian food like this.

PAN-SEARED CHICKEN CAPRESE

(2 servings)

½ cup olive oil
12-ounce chicken breast, pounded thin and cut in half
½ cup seasoned all-purpose flour
2 slices thinly sliced prosciutto
4 slices vine-ripe tomato
4 thin slices buffalo mozzarella
¾ cup chicken stock
1 cup baby spinach, washed
Balsamic reduction, as needed
Fresh basil, for garnish

Preheat oven to 400 degrees.

In a sauté pan, heat the oil over high heat. Dredge the chicken in the seasoned flour, then pan-sear the chicken until golden brown on both sides. Remove the chicken from the pan. Place the chicken in a baking dish.

Place 1 slice of prosciutto, 2 slices of tomato, and 2 slices of mozzarella on each breast.
Add the chicken stock to the dish. Bake the chicken in the 400-degree oven for 7 to 8 minutes.
Serve the chicken over the baby spinach. Drizzle with the balsamic reduction. Garnish with fresh basil. Serve immediately.

Chef's note: To make a balsamic reduction, combine 1 cup of sugar and 1 cup of balsamic vinegar in a saucepan over medium-high heat. Cook until mixture is reduced to a syrup.

Recommended wine: *Antinori Peppoli Chianti Classico*

Chef: Robert LaMoia

Owners: Bill Pinelli and
                   Steve Marra

Cuisine: Italian

Signature dish: Pappardelle

Price range: Appetizers,
                   $4 to $7

                   Entrees,
                   $9 to $14

Hours: Open seven days a week

        Monday through Thursday,
        5 to 9 pm

        Friday and Saturday,
        5 to 10 pm

        Sunday,
        noon to 8 pm

*In the Portuguese and Italian cultures, smelts are a delicacy.
If you've ever doubted this fact, try these and you'll be a believer.*

BOQUERONES
(PORTUGUESE-STYLE SMELTS)

(4 to 6 servings)

½ cup corn flour
⅓ cup wheat flour
1 tablespoons salt
1 egg
¼ cup milk
¾ cup water
3 cups cornflakes, unsweetened
2 pounds smelts, dressed
Vegetable oil, as needed for frying
2 to 3 tablespoons olive oil
1 tablespoon chopped garlic
½ teaspoon red pepper flakes
¼ to ½ cup sherry vinegar

In a large bowl, mix the corn and wheat flours with the salt. Beat in the egg and milk. Slowly add the water until the mixture resembles thin pancake batter.

In another bowl, crush the cornflakes into small pieces, but don't pulverize them.

Wash and dry the smelts thoroughly. Dip them in the batter, then roll them in the cornflakes. You can cook the smelts at this point, or refrigerate them or even freeze them for cooking at a later time.

In a deep pot, heat the vegetable oil to 360 degrees. Drop the smelts into the hot oil a few at a time. Do not overcrowd the pot. Cook until golden brown. Using a large slotted spoon, remove the smelts from the oil and drain them on paper towels.

Heat the olive oil in a large frying pan. Add the garlic and red pepper. Cook until mixture sizzles, but be careful not to burn the garlic as it will become bitter. Add the smelts to the pan and swirl them around to heat through. Add the sherry vinegar and carefully ignite, allowing the flames to subside and the vinegar to evaporate. Serve the smelts immediately.

Recommended wine: *Crios Torrontes*

This recipe is actually two fabulous dishes in one because it can exist on its own without the linguine. I love it both ways!

SCALLOPS FLORENTINE
(2 servings)

8 ounces (½ pound) scallops
2 tablespoons olive oil
1 tablespoon chopped garlic
Salt and pepper, to taste
½ cup diced tomatoes
4 cups baby spinach
¼ cup dry sherry
2 tablespoons heavy cream
12 tablespoons lemon butter
1 tablespoon garlic butter
½ cup shredded mozzarella
8 ounces cooked linguine

Preheat oven to 300 degrees.

In a large ovenproof frying pan, pan-sear the scallops in the oil. Add the garlic, salt and pepper to the pan. Add the diced tomatoes and spinach. Deglaze the pan with the sherry. Add the heavy cream, lemon butter and garlic butter. Reduce by one half. Sprinkle the mozzarella over the top of the scallops.

Place the pan in the 300-degree oven to melt the cheese. As soon as the cheese has melted, remove the pan from the oven. Pour the scallops over the cooked linguine. Serve immediately.

Chef's note: To make lemon butter, combine 1 stick of butter with the juice of a lemon. For this recipe, you will need to double those amounts. You'll have about 4 tablespoons left over which can be used to flavor other fish dishes, rice and pasta.

Recommended wine: *Ceretto Arneis*

PINELLI'S NORTH END CAFÉ

1058 Charles Street
North Providence, RI
401-726-4400
pinellimarrarestaurants.com

Chef: Andrew Juarez

Owners: Bill Pinelli and Steve Marra

Cuisine: Italian

Signature dish: Lasagna Bolognese

Price range: Appetizers, $5 to $9

Entrees, $14 to $22

Hours: Tuesday through Thursday, 4:30 to 10 pm

Friday and Saturday, 4:30 to 11 pm

Sunday, 3 to 9 pm

In Texas, almost every Mexican bakery sells huge layered sandwiches known as Tortas, according to Chef Andrew Juarez. This all fits into a "telera," a hard Mexican roll. The chef says it's a great snack, especially at the beach.

TORTAS (HARD ROLL MEXICAN SANDWICHES)

(6 servings)

6 telera or hard rolls such as Kaiser or French baguette
6 tablespoons refried beans (store-bought is fine)
Shredded cabbage, as needed
2 cups shredded chicken or pork
6 fried eggs
6 onion slices
6 tomato slices
6 avocado slices
6 slices goat cheese or feta cheese
6 thin strips chiles of your choice (Serrano, jalapeno, etc.)
6 tablespoons sour cream or crème fraiche
Salt and pepper, to taste
Fresh cilantro sprigs and freshly squeezed lime juice, optional

Slice each roll in half. Layer the bottom half of the roll with equal amounts of each ingredient, starting with the refried beans and ending with the sour cream. Season to taste with salt and pepper. Top with fresh cilantro and a squeeze of fresh lime juice, if desired. Serve immediately, or wrap in plastic wrap or aluminum foil for later.

Recommended beer: *Dos Equis Amber*

Here's a little known fact... I worked as the general manager here for four years long ago. It was then and still is one of the most unique dining spots in Rhode Island. A working U.S. Post Office for decades.

PAN-SEARED SEA SCALLOPS WITH FETTUCCINE
(2 servings)

¼ pound fettuccine pasta
6 large sea scallops
Salt and pepper, to taste
All-purpose flour, as needed
¼ cup extra virgin olive oil
1 small shallot, diced
1 teaspoon sliced garlic
4 sun-dried tomatoes
1 cup baby spinach
½ cup fish stock
1 teaspoon butter
2 tablespoons freshly chopped parsley

In a large pot of boiling salted water, cook the fettuccine until al dente.

Place a 12-inch sauté pan over medium-high heat. Season the sea scallops with salt and pepper, then dredge them in flour. Add the oil to the pan. Sear the scallops until golden brown on both sides. Add the shallots and garlic to the pan. Add the sun-dried tomatoes and spinach to the pan. Season lightly with salt and pepper. Cook for about 1 minute. Add the fish stock and bring to a boil.

Drain the pasta and place in a large heated serving bowl. Add the butter and parsley. Pour the sea scallop mixture over the cooked pasta and toss to coat well. Serve immediately.

Recommended wine: *Antinori Cervaro*

Chef:	Michael Gionti
Owner:	Pinelli-Marra Restaurant Group
Cuisine:	Regional Italian
Specialty:	Pasta and risotto
Price range:	Appetizers, $3 to $10
	Entrees, $10 to $25
Hours:	Sunday brunch, 10 am to 2 pm
	Tuesday through Thursday, 4:30 to 9:30 pm
	Friday and Saturday, 4:30 to 10:30 pm

POT AU FEU

44 Custom House Street
Providence, RI
401-273-8953
www.potaufeuri.com

Plan ahead on this one.

SUPREME DE CANETON ET CONFIT GIGOT BIGERADE (GRILLED DUCK BREAST AND DUCK LEG CONFIT)

(4 servings)

2 (5-pound) ducks, fresh if possible
1 tablespoon kosher salt
1 teaspoon sugar
4 fresh thyme sprigs
1 to 2 quarts duck fat

2 tablespoons sugar
2 tablespoons water
⅔ cup orange juice
⅛ cup red wine vinegar
¼ cup currant jelly
½ cup Port wine
1 pint duck stock
Salt and pepper, to taste
1 orange, cut into segments

Day 1: Remove the legs and breasts from the ducks. Roast the carcass of the duck in a hot oven until brown. Use this to make duck stock. You will need 1 to 2 pints of finished stock. Cook it for 7 to 8 hours. Strain through a fine mesh or cheesecloth.

Rub the legs with kosher salt, sugar and thyme. Refrigerate overnight.

Day 2: Rinse the legs under cold running water and pat dry. Simmer the duck legs in the duck fat at 200 degrees for 3 hours. This can be done in an oven set at approximately 250 degrees, or it can be done on the stovetop. Be careful — this can ignite if it gets too hot. Remove the legs with a slotted spoon and test for doneness. The legs should be extremely soft and almost falling off the bone.

While the legs are simmering in the duck fat, combine the sugar and water in a saucepan on high heat. When sugar caramelizes, carefully add orange juice, vinegar, currant jelly, Port wine and duck stock. Reduce to sauce consistency, which should take 30 minutes or longer.

Chef: John B. Richardson

Owners: Robert and Ann Burke

Cuisine: French

Signature dish: Pot au Feu

Price range: Appetizers, $7 to $15

Entrees, $17 to $34

Hours: Bistro is open for lunch Monday through Friday, 11:30 am to 2 pm, and for dinner, starting at 5:30 pm.

Salon is open for dinner Thursday and Friday, 6 to 9 pm, and Saturday, 6 to 9:30 pm.

You will need two days to prepare this classic French dish.

Preheat oven to 400 degrees. Season the duck breasts with salt and pepper. Grill or sear in a frying pan on the stovetop, skin side down. Turn over when the skin is golden brown and continue cooking until nicely colored on both sides. Remove from pan. Place the duck legs in the 400-degree oven for 5 to 10 minutes, then add the duck breast, skin side down. Cook until medium done.

Remove skin from breast. Place crisp duck leg on a plate. Slice the breast and arrange around the leg. Pour a little sauce over the breast only. Garnish with orange segments.

Recommended wine: *Lucien Lemoine Bourgogne Rouge*

Years ago when this stylish seafood house opened on Federal Hill, people said it was in the wrong location. Like I said years ago, what a great spot!

FRUTTI DI MARE (FRUIT OF THE SEA)

(4 servings)

1 tablespoon roasted garlic (must be done well in advance)*
½ cup olive oil
2 ounces Chilean sea bass
2 ounces swordfish
2 ounces salmon
12 mussels
4 littleneck clams
4 extra-large shrimp
1 tablespoon chopped shallots
½ cup white wine
8 ounces fresh linguine
1 cup marinara
2 tablespoons capers
2 tablespoons buerre monte

To roast the garlic, place 10 cloves in a baking dish, drizzle with a little olive oil, and bake at 275 degrees for 2 hours. Place the rest of the oil in a large frying pan over high heat. Pan sear all the seafood. Then add the shellfish to the pan. Add the shallots and roasted garlic. Deglaze the pan with the white wine. Cover the pan and simmer for 4 minutes.

Cook the fresh linguine in boiling salted water. Add the marinara to the large frying pan. Drain the pasta and add the pasta to the frying pan. Mix well with the marinara and other ingredients. Add the very end, add the capers and the buerre monte. Serve immediately.

Chef's note: Buerre monte is simply butter melted in a small amount of water. The water keeps the butterfat from breaking. The technique is simple and fail-safe. Simply heat a couple of tablespoons of water to the boil in a small saucepan. Add a stick of unsalted butter and reduce the heat to low.

Recommended wine: *Cakebread Sauvignon Blanc*

Just like it is here in the book, this restaurant is right next to its sister operation,
Providence Oyster Bar, on busy Atwells Avenue.
Prime location. Prime meats. Primetime!

BRAISED PRIME SHORT RIB

(1 serving)

1 (16-ounce) short rib
Salt and pepper, to taste
1 cup flour
½ cup olive oil
1 white onion, chopped
1 carrot, chopped
½ cup chopped celery
2 shallots, minced
8 garlic cloves, minced
4 thyme sprigs, chopped
4 rosemary sprigs, chopped
2 cups red wine
4 cups beef broth
½ cup demi glace (available in the gourmet soup section of supermarkets)

Preheat oven to 275 degrees.

Season the short rib with salt and pepper. Dust the short rib all over with flour. Get a large pot or Dutch oven very hot. Add the oil. Pan sear the short rib on all sides. Remove the short rib from the pot and set aside. Add all the vegetables, shallots, garlic and herbs to the pot. Deglaze the pan with red wine. Simmer and reduce for 10 minutes. Add the beef broth, demi glace and short rib. Cover the pot with a lid or aluminum foil. Place the pot in the 275-degree oven. Allow short rib to braise in the oven for 4 hours. Move the short rib from the pot to a serving dish. Cover with foil to keep warm. Pour all the ingredients from the pot into a blender and puree (this may have to be done in batches) to make a sauce. Serve the short rib with the sauce on the side.

Chef's note: This recipe can easily be doubled.

Recommended wine: *Joseph Phelps Cabernet*

RAPHAEL
BAR RISTO

1 Union Station
Providence, RI
401-421-4646
www.raphaelbarristo.com

Chef/Owner: Ralph Conte

Cuisine: New Age Italian

Specialty: Seafood

Signature dish: Lobster
Fra Diavolo

Price range: Appetizers,
$6 to $11

Entrees,
$14 to $29

Hours: Monday through Saturday,
5 pm to closing

Friday and Saturday,
5 pm to 2 am

My friend, Chef/Owner Ralph Conte, has been a master of award-winning cuisine in Rhode Island for more than a quarter of a century. Here's one example...

BLOCK ISLAND STRIPED BASS WITH BROWN BUTTER, CAPERS AND LEMON

(4 servings)

1 cup flour
2 tablespoons kosher salt
1 tablespoon black pepper
1 tablespoon cayenne pepper
1 tablespoon white pepper
4 (8-ounce) striped bass filets
¼ stick (2 tablespoons) butter
¼ cup capers
2 dozen caper berries
Juice from 1 lemon
½ cup white wine
½ stick (4 tablespoons) butter
¼ cup chopped fresh parsley
2 lemons, cut in half for garnish

Mix all dry ingredients. Dredge the fish in the flour mixture. Shake off excess flour. Heat a large heavy sauté pan. Add the butter; cook until brown and foaming. Place the fish in the pan. Cook until seared and dark brown, then turn over and repeat.

Lower heat to a simmer. Drain off all the butter. Add the capers, caper berries, lemon juice and wine. Allow to reduce for 5 minutes. Add ½ stick fresh butter. Place the fish on a serving platter. Cook the sauce for another 2 minutes. Add the parsley. Pour the sauce over the fish. Garnish with lemons and a parsley sprig.

Recommended wine: *Newton Unfiltered Red Label Chardonnay*

In the dining room with...

Jaime D'Oliveira,
Mill's Tavern and Red Stripe

Luciano Canova, Luciano's

Ralph Conte, Raphael Bar-Risto

Ezio Gentile, Sogno

Tina and Anthony Tomaselli, T's Restaurant

RASOI

727 East Avenue
Pawtucket, RI
401-728-5500
www.rasoi-restaurant.com

Chef/Owner: Sanjiv Dhar

Cuisine: Regional cuisines
                of India

Specialty: Three kinds of grilling
            — the tandoor clay oven,
            the charbroiler,
            and the flat-iron grill

Signature dish: Chicken Tikka
                   Lababdar

Price range: Appetizers,
                   $5 to $10

                   Entrees,
                   $10 to $20

Hours: Open seven days a week

                   Lunch on
            Monday through Friday,
               11:30 am to 3 pm

                   Dinner on
          Monday through Thursday,
               4:30 to 9:30 pm,
                   and Friday,
               4:30 to 10:30 pm

          Saturday, noon to 10:30 pm

          Sunday, noon to 9 pm

Rasoi means "kitchen" in India.

TANDOORI CHICKEN
(2 servings)

Marinade:
2 tablespoons plain yogurt, for marinating
2 tablespoons ginger paste
1 teaspoon red paprika
2 tablespoons garlic paste
2 tablespoons freshly squeezed lemon juice
½ teaspoon garam masala powder
2 tablespoons vegetable oil
Salt, to taste

1 (2-pound) chicken, rinsed and cut into pieces, skin removed
1 teaspoon red chili powder
1 tablespoon freshly squeezed lemon juice
Salt, to taste
Butter, as needed, melted for basting
Lemon wedges, for garnish
½ teaspoon chaat masala

Make the marinade by combining the yogurt, ginger paste, paprika, garlic paste, lemon juice, garam masala powder, oil and salt. Set aside.

With a sharp knife, make incisions into the leg and breast pieces. Combine the red chili powder, lemon juice and salt. Spread this mixture over the chicken pieces. In a large bowl, combine the chicken pieces with the marinade. Refrigerate for 3 to 4 hours.

Preheat oven to 375 degrees. Bake the chicken in the 375-degree oven for 15 minutes, turning the pieces once. Baste the chicken with the melted butter, and bake for another 5 minutes.

Remove the chicken from the oven, and place on a serving platter. Garnish with lemon wedges. Sprinkle with chaat masala.

Chef's note: Many of these ingredients, including the garam masala and the chaat masala, are available in Indian markets and spice shops.

Recommended wine: *Miner Viognier*

This flavorful dish will excite your tastebuds.

RED STRIPE

465 Angell Street
Providence, RI
401-437-6950

Chef: Matt Holmes

Owner: Jaime D'Oliveira

Cuisine: American Brasserie

Specialty: Comfort food

Signature dish: 10 different dishes featuring mussels

Price range: Appetizers, $4 to $12

Entrees, $9 to $24

Hours: Open seven days a week

Monday to Saturday, 11:30 am to 11 pm

Sunday, 9 am to 10 pm

Jamie D'Oliveira's "American Brasserie" is a Rhode Island hot spot for good reason — exciting comfort food like this.

MUSSELS WITH RED STRIPE BEER

(1 entrée serving, or 2 appetizer servings)

1 tablespoon olive oil
⅔ cup sliced shallots
1 tablespoon chopped garlic
⅔ cup halved cherry tomatoes
½ pound Prince Edward Island mussels, cleaned and debearded
1 cup Red Stripe beer
1 cup heavy cream
1 teaspoon salt
1 pinch pepper
6 tablespoons pesto

First, select a pan large enough to accommodate the mussels, keeping in mind that when opened, the mussels will take up twice as much space. The pan you choose should be at least one gallon and have a lid.

Place the pan on high heat and warm it up for 30 to 60 seconds. Add the oil to the pan. Add the sliced shallots and cook for 15 to 20 seconds. Add the garlic and cherry tomatoes. Stir to mix well. Add the mussels. Stir to mix well. Add the beer, heavy cream, salt and pepper. Cover and cook until all the mussels are open. About 2 minutes after you add the liquids to the pot, it helps to stir the mussels one time during the cooking.

When all the mussels are open, stir in the pesto and serve immediately.

Chef's note: Enjoy this dish with crusty bread or French fries.

This restaurant oozes rustic New England charm,
yet the menu is as cosmopolitan as can be. Here's some evidence.

REMINGTON HOUSE INN

3376 Post Road
Warwick, RI
401-736-8388
theremingtonhouseinn.com

PAN-BRAISED COD IN A SPICY CHORIZO AND SPINACH RED SAUCE

(4 servings)

4 tablespoons olive oil, divided
Salt and black pepper, to taste
Flour, as needed for dusting
4 (6-ounce) cod filets (or any other white fish)
1 small white onion, diced
2 garlic cloves, minced
½ pound chorizo, sliced lengthwise and cut into ¼-inch pieces
1 teaspoon dried oregano
1 teaspoon dried basil
1 (10-ounce) can diced tomatoes, with juice
1 cup low-sodium chicken broth
1 tablespoon tomato paste
1 pound baby spinach
2 tablespoons chopped parsley

Preheat a large sauté pan over medium-high heat. Add 2 tablespoons of oil to the heated pan. Lightly salt, pepper and flour each side of the cod filets. Shake off excess flour. Place the cod into the pan. Sear the first side for 2 minutes, or until golden brown. Flip over and sear the second side for another 2 minutes. Move the fish to a warm holding plate.

Add the remaining oil to the pan. Add the onions, garlic and chorizo. Sauté for 4 minutes, or until onions are soft and translucent. Add the oregano, basil, tomatoes, chicken broth and tomato paste. Bring mixture to a boil and reduce to a simmer. Simmer for 10 minutes. Add the fish back to the sauce, and simmer another 5 minutes, or until fish starts to flake. Add the spinach and parsley to the sauce. Simmer for 1 minute. Season to taste with salt and pepper. Pour the sauce over and around the fish. Serve over garlic mashed potatoes or rice, if desired.

Recommended wine: *Vietti Barbera D'Asti*

Chef:	Clifton J. Cameron
Owners:	Michael and Patrick Berek
Cuisine:	American-Italian
Specialty:	Sautéed pasta and grilled meats
Signature dish:	Chicken Mascarpone Pasta
Price range:	Appetizers, $6 to $9
	Entrees, $14 to $18
Hours:	Sunday through Thursday, 4 to 10 pm
	Friday and Saturday, 4 to 11 pm

RISTORANTE VIA ROMA

1861 Smith Street
North Providence, RI
401-349-3350
www.viaromari.com

Chefs: Domenic Ierfino and
Vincenzo Zarone

Owners: Domenic Ierfino,
Vincenzo Zarone, Sisto Grillo
and Alessandro Qualiozzi

Cuisine: Italian

Specialty: Pasta, veal, seafood
and steaks

Signature dish: Filetto di Pesce
alla Romana

Price range: Appetizers,
$7 to $13

Entrees,
$17 to $30
(and some at market price)

Hours: Open seven days a week

Lunch,
Monday through Friday,
11:30 am to 2:30 pm

Dinner,
Monday through Saturday,
4:30 to 10 pm

Sunday brunch,
10 am to 2 pm

When I prepared this wonderful recipe, I put on one of my favorite Dean Martin songs, "On an Evening in Roma," and toasted the food and the mood. Try it!

FILETTO DI PESCE ALLA ROMANA (FILLET OF FISH, ROMAN STYLE)

(1 serving)

Olive oil, as needed
½ Bermuda onion, sliced
Pinch of fresh minced garlic
2 fresh ripe tomatoes, peeled and diced
12 kalamata olives, pitted
Sea salt and coarsely ground black pepper, to taste
8 to 10 ounces fresh local scrod
¾ cup white wine
Fish stock or clam juice, as needed
12 capers
¼ teaspoon saffron
4 littleneck clams
4 mussels
4 large sea scallops
4 large shrimp, peeled and deveined, tail left on
Fresh parsley, for garnish

In a heavy sauté pan, heat enough olive oil to coat the bottom of the pan. Add onions, garlic, diced tomatoes, olives, salt and pepper. Simmer for about 5 minutes. Add the scrod, white wine and a ladle of fish stock. Cover and simmer for about 5 minutes. Add the capers, saffron, clams and mussels. Cover and simmer for about 3 minutes. Add the scallops and shrimp, and cook for another 4 minutes. Add more fish stock, if needed. You should have a broth-like consistency.

Place the cooked scrod on a dinner plate. Surround the fish with the cooked clams, mussels, scallops and shrimp. Top the fish with the saffron, tomato and onion broth. Drizzle just a little olive oil on top. Garnish with fresh parsley.

Recommended wine: *Regillo Frascati Superiore*

Spending some quality in-studio time with little Dino.
Now, "that's amore!"

RODIZIO STEAKHOUSE

1195 Douglas Avenue
North Providence, RI
401-354-8411
www.rodiziosteakhouseri.com

Chef/Owner: Nick Iannuccilli

Cuisine: Brazilian steakhouse
with Italian flair

Specialty: Meats on skewers

Signature dish: Rotisserie Filet
Mignon

Price range: All you can eat
for $26.99 per person

Antipasto island only,
$19.99 per person

Children half price

Hours: Open seven days a week

Monday through Saturday,
4:30 pm to closing

Sunday,
noon to closing

In July and August, the hours on
Sunday are 4:30 pm to closing.

I like the fact that the olive oil acts as a tenderizer

ROTISSERIE-STYLE FILET MIGNON
(8 to 12 servings)

1 whole prime beef filet mignon, 5 to 6 pounds, trimmed
¼ cup extra virgin olive oil
3 tablespoons sea salt
Freshly ground black pepper, to taste

Evenly coat the entire filet mignon with the olive oil, then season with the salt and pepper. Place the entire filet mignon lengthwise on a rotisserie-style skewer. Place the skewer over a hot flame (500 degrees), and rotate continuously. Cook for 10 to 14 minutes for medium-rare (longer for medium-well or well-done). Carve the meat tableside. Serve with your favorite condiments.

Recommended wine: *Terrabianca Campaccio*

Rodízio
STEAKHOUSE
"Feast your fill from Milan to Brazil."

Chef Nick

...and helps to seal in the juices. Nick can cook!

RUE DE L'ESPOIR

99 Hope Street
Providence, RI
401-751-8890
www.therue.com

*Rhode Island "foodies in the know" speak of 'The Rue' in glowing terms.
Now, you will too... simple, creative and delicious!*

CHICKEN ARTICHOKE BREAD SALAD
(6 servings)

6 boneless skinless chicken breasts
½ cup olive oil
2 teaspoons lemon juice
1 bunch cilantro, chopped
Salt and pepper, to taste
½ loaf ciabatta bread or another good crusty bread
½ cup olive oil mixed with salt, pepper, oregano, rosemary and thyme
½ cup shredded parmesan cheese
16-ounce can artichoke hearts, marinated in olive oil, garlic, salt, pepper and oregano
16-ounce can sliced black olives
1 bunch fresh asparagus, blanched and cut into bite-size pieces
1 cup oven-roasted tomatoes*

Preheat oven to 375 degrees. Combine the chicken breasts with the olive oil, lemon juice, cilantro, salt and pepper. Roast the chicken breasts in the 375-degree oven for 20 minutes. Cut the roasted chicken into bite-size cubes.

Cut the bread into 1-inch cubes. Toss the cubes with the seasoned olive oil, parmesan cheese, salt and pepper. Spread the bread cubes on a baking sheet pan, and roast in the 375-degree oven until golden brown.

In a very large bowl, combine the roasted chicken cubes, bread cubes, marinated artichoke hearts, sliced black olives, asparagus, and roasted tomatoes. Mix well but gently. Serve immediately.

*To roast the tomatoes, slice the tomatoes. Toss the slices with olive oil, salt and pepper. Place the tomatoes on a baking sheet pan. Slow roast the tomatoes in a preheated 200-degree oven for 4 hours.

Recommended wine: *Mastroberardino Greco di Tufo*

Chef: Michael Koussa

Owner: Deborah Norman

Cuisine: American Bistro

Price range: Appetizers,
                 $8 to $12

                 Entrees,
                 $13 to $30

Hours: Open seven days a week
         for breakfast, brunch,
         lunch, and dinner.

We don't know who Loretta is, but one taste of this dish told us she is a great cook.

SARDELLA'S ITALIAN RESTAURANT

30 Memorial Boulevard
Newport, RI
401-849-6312
www.sardellas.com

VEAL SCALOPPINE LORETTA

(2 servings)

12 veal medallions, ¼-inch thick (approximately 1 and ¾ pounds)
Salt and pepper, to taste
Flour, as needed
2 tablespoons olive oil
4 ounces sliced pancetta
¼ cup sliced onions
¼ cup sliced mushrooms
¼ cup brandy
¾ cup veal stock
2 tablespoons butter

Season the veal medallions with salt and pepper, and dust them with flour. In a medium-size sauté pan, over moderately high heat, add the olive oil. Sauté the veal in the oil for 2 minutes per side. Remove the veal from the pan to complete the sauce.

Add the pancetta and onions to the pan. Sauté until transparent. Add the mushrooms and veal. Add the brandy, and ignite carefully. Allow the brandy to burn off. Add the veal stock and butter. Cook the sauce for 2 minutes, allowing it to reduce and thicken. Serve immediately over your favorite pasta.

Recommended wine: *Ars Poetica Aglianico Riserva*

Chef: Kevin Fitzgerald

Owners: Richard Sardella and
              Patrick Fitzgerald

Cuisine: Northern and
              Southern Italian

Specialty: Veal and pasta dishes

Signature dish: Scaloppine Loretta

Price range: Appetizers,
                  $10 to $13

                    Entrees,
                  $14 to $25

Hours: Open seven days a week

        Monday through Saturday,
              5 to 10 pm

                    Sunday,
              4 to 10 pm

SAVINI'S

476 Rathbun Street
Woonsocket, RI
401-762-5114

If only these walls could talk. Back in the 1950s, this was a thriving Sons of Italy lodge. The tradition continues today with this restaurant serving authentic Italian food.

PORKETTA
(6 servings)

1 boneless pork butt, approximately 7 pounds
Whole garlic cloves, as many as you desire
Black pepper, oregano, basil and fennel seed, to taste
Olive oil, as needed

Preheat oven to 450 degrees.

Pork butts are fatty as a rule, so plan on shrinkage. Split the butt open. Make 7 deep cuts into the meat, with the fatty side down. Fill the deep cuts with whole garlic cloves. Sprinkle the entire butt with generous amounts of pepper, oregano, basil and fennel seed. Roll the butt up like a jelly roll, and tie with butcher's twine.

Place the butt fatty side down in a roasting pan containing about 1 inch of water blended with a little oil. Place the pan in the preheated oven, and cook for 30 minutes. Decrease the oven temperature to 350 degrees, and cook for another 2 hours. Decrease the temperature to 250 degrees, and cook for another 3 to 4 hours. After 4 hours of cooking, turn the butt over. If the water and oil evaporate, add more to keep the meat moist.

Chef's note: Serve the porketta with roasted red bliss potatoes that have been seasoned with salt, pepper and rosemary and cooked for 1 hour at 325 degrees in a pan with the oil from the porketta pan. This porketta is also great served with penne pasta and salad.

Recommended wine: *Kaesler Stonehorse GSM*

Chef/Owner: Roger Savini

Cuisine: Italian

Specialty: Steaks and seafood

Signature dish: Family-Style
                         Chicken

Price range: Appetizers,
                       $3 to $9

                         Entrees,
                       $6 to $19

Hours: Sunday,
                   noon to 9 pm

          Tuesday through Thursday,
                       4 to 9 pm

             Friday and Saturday,
                   11 am to 10 pm

One of our favorite recipes in this book. Perfect for your next dinner party.
Who knew chicken could taste so heavenly?

SHELT
HARBOR

10 Wagner Road
Westerly, RI
401-322-8883
www.shelterharborinn.com

HAZELNUT CHICKEN WITH ORANGE-FRANGELICO CREAM
(2 to 4 servings)

1 large orange (or 1 can mandarin oranges)
2 whole boneless chicken breasts, skinned and halved
⅓ cup finely chopped toasted hazelnuts
½ cup fresh bread crumbs
¼ tablespoon finely chopped thyme
Flour seasoned with salt and pepper, as needed
1 egg, beaten with 1 tablespoon water
3 tablespoons unsalted butter
1 cup heavy cream
½ cup orange juice
2 tablespoons Frangelico liqueur
2 teaspoons finely chopped fresh thyme
Salt and pepper, to taste

Remove the peel and white pith from the orange. Cut between the membranes with a small sharp knife to release orange segments. Or you can used canned mandarin oranges. Set aside.

Using a meat mallet or rolling pin, pound the chicken between 2 sheets of waxed paper to a thickness of about ¼ inch. On a large plate, combine the hazelnuts, bread crumbs and thyme. Dredge the chicken in the flour, shaking off excess. Dip the chicken into the beaten egg, then into the hazelnut mixture, shaking off excess.

In a heavy skillet over medium heat, melt the butter. Add the chicken, and cook until golden brown and springy to the touch, about 3 minutes per side. If the chicken breasts are thick, finish cooking in a preheated 350-degree oven. Transfer the cooked chicken to a serving platter. Cover with foil to keep warm.

Into the same skillet, combine the cream, orange juice, liqueur and remaining thyme. Bring to a boil, stirring constantly until slightly thickened. Season with salt and pepper. Add the orange sections. Spoon the sauce over the chicken, and serve immediately, garnished with fresh thyme sprigs.

Chef: Edward Gencarelli

Owner: James T. Dey

Cuisine: Creative American

Specialty: Country inn experience

Signature dish: Hazelnut Chicken
    with Orange-Thyme Cream

Price range: Appetizers,
        $6 to $11

        Entrees,
        $14 to $25

Hours: Open seven days a week
    from 7:30 am to 10 pm.

Recommended wine: *J. Bookwalter Riesling*

Chef: Christopher Ferris

Owner: Newport Harbor Group

Cuisine: Genuine barbecue

Specialty: Outdoor dining in
the heart of Newport

Price range: Appetizers,
$4.25 to $24.95

Entrees,
$7.50 to $25.95

Hours: Seasonal; open from
mid-May to mid-October

Monday through Thursday,
11:30 am to 10 pm

Friday and Saturday,
11:30 am to 11 pm

Sunday,
noon to 10 pm

*What a sensational fresh recipe! You're cooking crabs, plucking the corn right off the ears.
And then there's the rum!*

CORN AND CRAB CHOWDER WITH MOUNT GAY RUM
(4 to 6 servings)

12 Jonah crabs
6 ears of corn, smoked over a real hickory wood fire
2 cups diced potatoes, ¼-inch in size
1 cup finely diced onions
½ cup finely diced celery
¼ pound butter (1 stick)
1 cup flour
½ gallon half-and-half, warmed slightly
2 tablespoons Outerbridge Sherry Pepper Sauce
2 tablespoons Mount Gay Rum
Paprika, to garnish

In a large stockpot, cook the crabs in a gallon of water. Remove the crabs when cooked, and reduce the liquid to 1 quart to make crab stock. When the crabs are cool, pick the crabmeat to be used later (they should yield 1 pound of meat).

Remove the corn from the smoked ears of corn. Set the smoked corn aside.

Cook the potatoes in boiling water until al dente; drain and shock with cold water.

In a large frying pan, sauté the onions and celery in the butter over low heat until tender. Add the flour to make a roux; cook over low heat for 2 to 3 minutes. Add the roux and sautéed vegetables to the crab stock. Add the corn, potatoes, tempered half-and-half, sherry pepper sauce, rum and crabmeat. Cook over medium heat until potatoes are tender. Serve immediately in warm soup bowls. Garnish each serving with paprika.

In Italian, sogno means dream, and chef/owner Ezio Gentile's rich, flavorful creation is a pasta lover's dream for sure.

FARFALLE DEL SOGNO

(2 servings)

1 pound farfalle pasta
½ cup chopped leeks
1 cup sliced portabello mushrooms
1 tablespoon butter
2 tablespoons Marsala wine
1 cup heavy cream
6 ounces prosciutto di Parma, diced
¼ cup grated Parmigiano Reggiano cheese

In a pot of boiling salted water, cook the pasta until al dente.

In a large frying pan, sauté the leeks and mushrooms in the butter. Add the wine. Add the cream. Bring to a boil, and simmer until the cream reduces to a thick sauce. Add the diced prosciutto. Drain the pasta, and add it to the frying pan, tossing to coat well. Sprinkle the cheese over all the pasta. Serve immediately.

Recommended wine: *Poggio Antico Rosso di Montalcino*

TABLE 28

28 Water Street
East Greenwich, RI
401-885-1170
www.table28.com

Chef: Gene Allsworth

Owner: Gary Marinosci

Cuisine: Nouvelle American,
Asian and Italian

Signature dish: Braised Angus
Beef Short Ribs

Price range: Appetizers,
$8 to $10

Entrees,
$16 to $24

Hours: Open seven days a week

In the summer,
from noon to 10 pm

In the winter,
from 5 to 10 pm

Chef Gene Allsworth's recipe is quick, easy, and so delish!
One bite and you'll be transported to the East Greenwich Marina boarding
your yacht as the crowd at Table 28 watches with envy.

THAI-STYLE CRAB CAKES

(6 servings)

2 eggs
½ cup mayonnaise
½ tablespoon kosher salt
½ teaspoon white pepper
Dash of Worcestershire sauce
1 tablespoon sweet Thai chili sauce (available in Asian markets)
1 tablespoon freshly squeezed lemon juice
1 tablespoon freshly chopped basil
1 (1-pound) can pasteurized lump crabmeat
2 cups panko or Japanese bread crumbs
Olive oil, as needed

In a large mixing bowl, combine the eggs, mayonnaise, salt, pepper, Worcestershire sauce, chili sauce, lemon juice and fresh basil. Add the crabmeat and bread crumbs. Toss together until well combined. Form crab cakes using an ice cream scoop, or use your hands to make patties.

Preheat oven to 350 degrees.

In a nonstick skillet, heat a little olive oil. Cook the patties until brown on both sides. Finish cooking the crab cakes in the 350-degree oven for about 5 minutes, or until the center is hot. Serve immediately.

Recommended wine: *J Vineyard Pinot Gris*

Do you have an adventurous palate? Then try this recipe.
You will be deliciously rewarded for your efforts.
Ten has always been one of Southern New England's best for sushi.

SUSHI SANDWICH
(1 serving)

1 nori sheet, 4x6 inches in size
6 ounces prepared sushi rice
1 ounce yellowtail
1 ounce salmon
1 ounce yellowfin tuna
1 ounce truffle oil
1 teaspoon masago (flying fish roe)
Spicy mayonnaise (equal amounts of Japanese mayonnaise and sriracha chili sauce)

Lay a nori sheet shiny side up on a sanitized work surface. Press 5 ounces of the sushi rice on the nori. Cover thoroughly. Flip over the sheet so the long way runs horizontally. Press the remaining sushi rice in a square in the middle of the sheet. Lay the various types of fish next to one another on the square. Fold the nori from right to left to the center. Then fold left to right. You should end up with a square. Press together and seal the sides using both hands. Rub with the truffle oil and masago. Cut the sushi sandwich from corner to corner, making triangle shapes. Serve face up showing all the layers of the fish. Drizzle each piece with the spicy mayonnaise.

Chef's note: All these ingredients can be found in Asian markets. Most sushi products can now be found in grocery stores. Questions? Contact the chef at chefseanmccabe@aol.com.

Recommended wine: *Fantinel Prosecco*

Save this one for a cold winter night. It will warm your heart and soul.

MOROCCAN LAMB STEW

(6 servings)

2-pound leg of lamb, cut into 1-inch cubes
Salt and pepper, to taste
½ cup olive oil
1 large onion, chopped
2 large carrots, chopped
2 celery stalks, chopped
⅓ cup red wine
1 cup beef broth
3 plum tomatoes, peeled, or 1 small can plum tomatoes
1 teaspoon each: dried basil, dried oregano, coriander, paprika, cumin
½ teaspoon each: cardamom, curry powder
2 teaspoons turmeric
2 bay leaves
1 pound chickpeas
Couscous, plain yogurt and fresh cilantro, as needed

Season the lamb cubes with salt and pepper. Heat the olive oil in a large pot. Quickly sear the lamb cubes. Add the onion, carrots and celery. Cook until the onion is translucent. Add the red wine, beef broth, tomatoes, spices and herbs. Simmer for 1 hour, or until the lamb is tender. Adjust the seasoning to taste. Add the chickpeas. Cook for another 10 minutes. Serve over couscous. Garnish with yogurt and freshly chopped cilantro.

Recommended wine: *Alamos Malbec*

Don't ever tell my good friend Tony Papa that he gives you too much. He'll only laugh and say "Not too much for me! "... and that's why he is one of my favorites.

ZUPPA DI PESCE (FISH SOUP)

(4 servings)

18 littleneck clams

12 mussels

1 and ½ pounds jumbo white shrimp

2 pounds fresh fish (striped bass and cod)

¼ cup olive oil

1 cup chopped white onions

4 garlic cloves, chopped

½ teaspoon crushed hot pepper flakes

½ teaspoon fennel seed

1 teaspoon dried thyme (or 1 and ½ teaspoons fresh thyme)

2 teaspoons dried basil

1 teaspoon saffron, crumbled

Sea salt and freshly ground black pepper, to taste

¼ cup white wine

4 fresh tomatoes, peeled, chopped and seeded (or canned tomatoes, peeled and pureed)

Scrub the clams and mussels under cold running water. Shell and devein the shrimp. Cut the fish into bite-size chunks. Set aside.

In a large saucepan, heat the oil. Add the chopped onions. Cook until wilted. Add the garlic, hot pepper flakes, fennel, thyme, basil, saffron, salt and pepper. Deglaze the pan with the wine. Add the tomatoes, and bring to a boil. Lower the heat, cover and simmer for 10 minutes. Add the clams and mussels. Simmer for 10 minutes. Add the shrimp and striped bass. Simmer for 10 minutes. Add the cod, partly cover, and simmer for 10 to 20 minutes, or until the shellfish opens and the shrimp is pink.

Chef's note: This is excellent served over rice or pasta, especially capellini with a drizzle of extra virgin olive oil from Umbria, Italy, and a generous sprinkling of freshly grated Pecorino Romano cheese. On the side, serve broccoli rabe aglio olio and crusty Italian bread.

Recommended wine: *Terre Dora Falanghina*

Fried calamari is delicious, but real "squid" aficionados will judge you on your squid sauce. This one's a winner.

LINGUINE WITH SQUID SAUCE
(2 to 4 servings)

1 and ½ cups fresh calamari rings
5 tablespoons extra virgin olive oil
2 garlic cloves
1 to 2 teaspoons crushed red pepper flakes, more or less to taste
1 cup white wine, preferably Pinot Grigio
3 cups tomato sauce
2 fresh oregano sprigs
3 fresh basil leaves
1 pound linguine
Basil leaves, as needed

In a medium-size saucepan over medium-high heat, combine the calamari, oil, garlic and red pepper flakes. Cook for 6 minutes or until the calamari starts to sizzle. Remove from the heat, and add the wine, tomato sauce and oregano. Return the pan to the stove, and simmer for 2 to 3 minutes, stirring frequently. The calamari should be extremely tender and can easily be cut with a fork. If the sauce continues to cook down, add a little hot pasta water to keep the calamari submerged in the sauce.

Bring a large pot of salted water to a boil. Cook the linguine for 6 to 8 minutes or until al dente. Drain the linguine, and immediately add it to the simmering calamari, tossing to coat well. Divide the pasta equally between 2 plates (if you're really hungry). Serve at once with torn basil leaves sprinkled over the top of the linguine.

Recommended wine: *Deforville Dolcetto D'Alba*

At the table, indoors
and al fresco, with...

Mike Degnan, Providence Oyster Bar
and Providence Prime

Carlo Slaughter and Denis Thibeault, D. Carlo Trattoria

Chris Spertini, Costantino's Ristorante

Marc Whitehead, Table 28

Aaron Edwards, Trattoria del Corso

T'S RESTAURANT

1059 Park Avenue
Cranston, RI
401-946-5900
www.tsrestaurantri.com

Chef: Anthony Tomaselli

Owners: Anthony and
     Tina Tomaselli

Cuisine: Breakfast, lunch, catering

Specialty: Filling your stomach
     and your soul

Signature dish: Rose Window
     Waffle, Red Chowder,
     Escarole and Bean Soup

Price range: Breakfast,
     $5 to $10

     Lunch,
     $6 to $9

Hours: Open seven days a week
     for breakfast and lunch,
     from 6:30 am to 3 pm.

My good friends, Anthony and Tina, own wha

CHARBROILED ITALIAN-STYLE CHICKEN PANINI

(3 to 6 servings)

Chicken Marinade:
 1 cup olive oil
 1 tablespoon chopped fresh garlic
 1 tablespoon Worcestershire sauce
 1 tablespoon teriyaki sauce
 1 tablespoon chopped parsley
 1 teaspoon Cajun seasoning
 1 teaspoon salt
 Pinch freshly ground pepper

3 chicken boneless chicken breasts,
 slightly pounded

T's Famous Focaccia Bread:
 Olive oil, as needed
 Salt and pepper, to taste
 Rosemary, to taste
 Garlic powder, to taste
 1 pound bread dough, made from scratch or
  purchased at supermarkets and bakeries
 Parsley, as needed

Olive Spread:
 1 cup Hellman's mayonnaise
 1 cup softened cream cheese
 ½ cup olive tapenade
 Salt and pepper, to taste

Roasted Red Peppers:
 3 red peppers
 Olive oil, as needed
 Salt and pepper, to taste
 Garlic powder, to taste

Freshly baked focaccia
Olive spread
1 head green leaf lettuce
Roma tomatoes, sliced
Roasted red peppers
Freshly shredded mozzarella cheese

In a large bowl, combine all the marinade ingredients. (Or use your favorite bottled Italian marinade.) Marinate the chicken in the marinade for 24 hours in the refrigerator.

Coat the bottom of a half sheet pan or cookie sheet with olive oil, and sprinkle with the salt, pepper, rosemary and garlic powder. Stretch the bread dough to create a 4x12-inch rectangle. Place the dough in the oiled pan, and coat with more oil, salt, pepper, rosemary and parsley. Set the pan aside for approximately 1 hour, and allow the dough to rise about 2 inches. Bake in a preheated 375-degree oven for 15 minutes. Rotate the pan in the oven, and bake for approximately 25 additional minutes, to desired crustiness. This will make 3 pieces of focaccia, 4x4 inches in size. (Or purchase soft Italian rolls at your local bakery.)

In a bowl, combine all the olive spread ingredients. (Or purchase olive spread from the gourmet section of markets.)

I affectionately call "Rhode Island's Neighborhood Restaurant" with an incredible menu to feed the palate and special atmosphere that feeds the soul.

Wash the red peppers. Cut into strips of a desired width. Remove all seeds. Place the pepper strips in a large bowl. Coat with the olive oil. Season with salt, pepper and garlic powder. Place the strips in a baking pan, and roast for 20 to 25 minutes in a preheated 350-degree oven. (Or purchase roasted red peppers from the Italian section of your supermarket.)

To prepare the sandwich:
Charbroil or sauté the marinated chicken breasts until done. Slice the focaccia horizontally in half, creating a top and bottom slice. Spread 2 tablespoons of olive spread on the bottom slice of focaccia. Layer a desired amount of lettuce, tomatoes, roasted red peppers and shredded mozzarella on top of the olive spread. Top with the cooked chicken. Cover with the top slice of focaccia. Place the sandwich in a panini grill, and cook according to the manufacturer's directions. (Or head to T's Restaurant in Cranston, and we'll do it for you!)

Chef's note: Add a side of freshly made pasta salad. Yum!

TUCKER'S BISTRO

150 Broadway
Newport, RI
401-846-3449
www.tuckersbristro.com

Owners: Tucker Harris and
                   Ellen Retlev

Cuisine: Eclectic/Fusion

Specialty: Bistro dishes

Price range: Appetizers,
                         $8 to $11

                         Entrees,
                   $20 to $32

Hours: Open seven days a week
                for dinner,
                6 to 10 pm,
          and on weekends,
             6 to 10:30 pm

*This recipe may be a bit labor intensive, but the results are definitely worth it.
Our taste testers were moaning with delight after just one bite.*

THAI SHRIMP NACHOS

Sauce:

    1 tablespoon vegetable oil
    1 tablespoon grated ginger root
    1 tablespoon chopped garlic
    1 tablespoon chopped shallots
    Small bunch of lemon grass (if you have it)
    1 cup sake or white wine
    2 tablespoons Thai red curry paste
    1 quart heavy cream
    1 can coconut milk
    1 can condensed milk

1 package wonton wrappers
Oil, as needed for deep frying
2 dozen shrimp
2 leeks, sliced
2 bunches scallions (green part only)
2 red peppers, cut into thin julienne strips

In a heavy saucepan, heat the oil. Add the ginger root, garlic, shallots and lemon grass. Cook until tender. Deglaze the pan with the sake or wine. Whisk in the red curry paste. Add the heavy cream, and reduce by half. Add the coconut milk, and reduce again. Add the condensed milk. Keep warm.

Cut the wonton wrappers in half diagonally and deep fry in hot oil until crisp. Drain on paper towels.

In a large frying pan, sauté the shrimp, leeks, scallions and peppers. Pour over fried wontons, and add the Thai sauce. Serve immediately.

Close your eyes. Sea breezes and summertime in Newport. Sunshine. Bowen's Wharf. And there you are with a steaming pot of littlenecks in front of you along with your favorite beverage... this is livin'. I love eating food without silverware!

STEAMED LITTLENECKS WITH CHORIZO

(1 serving)

¼ pound chorizo, diced or crumbled into small bits
¼ cup fennel, diced
1 small vine ripe tomato, diced
10 littleneck clams
½ cup white wine
½ cup clam juice
1 slice Tuscan bread

In a sauté pan, slowly cook the chorizo until brown. Add the fennel, tomatoes and littlenecks. Cook for a 2 to 3 minutes over high heat to combine the flavors. Reduce the heat. Add the white wine and clam juice. Cover the pan and simmer until the clams open. Discard clams that do not open. Transfer the clams and broth to a serving bowl. Serve immediately with warm Tuscan bread.

Chef's note: This recipe can easily be doubled. Simply figure on the above ingredients per person, and use a larger sauté pan.

Recommended wine: *Shafer Red Shoulder Ranch Chardonnay*

TWIN HEARTH BUFFET AT TWIN RIVER

100 Twin River Road
Lincoln, RI
401-723-3200
www.twinriver.com

Pastry Chef: Jim Ungiran

Owner: BLB Investors

Cuisine: American/International

Specialty: All-you-can-eat buffet

Price range: From 11 am to 4 pm,
              $13.95 per person

              After 4 pm,
              $16.95 per person

Hours: Open seven days a week

        Sunday through Thursday,
        11 am to 10 pm

        Friday and Saturday,
        11 am to midnight

Long before all of the trendy new desserts, there were simple, delicious recipes like this one, the classic of all classics. Food this good will never go out of style.

BREAD PUDDING

(4 to 8 servings)

8 eggs
¾ cup sugar
3 cups half-and-half
1 cup heavy cream
1 tablespoon cinnamon
¼ cup golden raisins
¼ cup melted butter
1 and ½ pounds day-old white bread (about 1 loaf), sliced
Whipped cream, fresh mint and powdered sugar, as needed for garnish

Preheat oven to 350 degrees.

In a large mixing bowl, combine the eggs, sugar, half-and-half, and heavy cream. Mix until the sugar is dissolved. Stir in the cinnamon — the mixture should turn into a custard consistency. Place the golden raisins and melted butter on the bottom of 11x9-inch baking pan. Add the sliced bread and cover with the custard. Place the baking pan inside another slightly larger pan that has been filled partially with water to create a water bath. Bake for 45 minutes to 1 hour or until the custard sets. Allow to cool for 30 minutes before serving. Garnish with whipped cream and fresh mint, and dust with powdered sugar to finish the plate.

Chef's note: For a more elegant and richer version, brioche could be used in place of white bread.

I grew up in this restaurant. I have great affection for the DeAngelus family. Twin Oaks is a Rhode Island dining icon since 1933 because of sensational recipes like this one.

BAKED STUFFED SHRIMP

(16 to 20 servings)

5 pounds jumbo shrimp, 10 count per pound or larger
2 pounds butter
1 garlic clove, chopped
2 tablespoons chopped parsley
1 and ¾ pounds round buttery crackers, ground fine
¼ pound fine bread crumbs

Peel the shrimp, split the underside, and remove the black vein. Set the shrimp aside.

In a large saucepan, melt the butter over medium-high heat. Add the garlic, and sauté for 5 minutes. Remove the garlic before it turns brown. Add the parsley, cracker crumbs and bread crumbs. Mix well.

Preheat oven to 400 degrees.

Place the shrimp on an ungreased baking sheet. Spoon the stuffing mixture into the split underside of each shrimp. Bake in the 400-degree oven for 15 minutes. Serve immediately.

Recommended wine: *Luca Chardonnay*

100 Sab...
Cranston, R1
401-781-0699
www.twinoaksrest.com

Chef: Bill Smith

Owners: Susan DeAngelus-Valles, William DeAngelus III, James DeAngelus, Patricia Hathaway-DeAngelus, and Kathleen Fiske

Cuisine: American and Italian

Specialty: Black Angus steaks

Signature dish: Baked Stuffed Shrimp and Veal Parmigiana

Price range: Appetizers, $4 to $8

Entrees, $10 to $26

Hours: Tuesday to Sunday, 11:30 am to closing

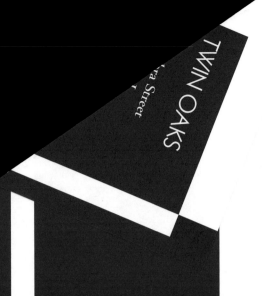
Chef: Basil Rockwell

Owners: Bill Pinelli and Steve Marra

Cuisine: American Eclectic

Specialty: Asian and American influenced cooking

Signature dish: Sesame Ahi Tuna

Price range: Appetizers, $6 to $9

Entrees, $13 to $18

Hours: Open seven days a week

Sunday through Thursday, 11:30 am to 10 pm

Wednesday through Saturday, 11:30 am to midnight

This is an exciting and flavorful "Twist" on pork loin.
The aromas will fill your kitchen. It's a beautiful thing!

APPLE CIDER/MAPLE GLAZED PORK TENDERLOIN
(2 servings)

I pork tenderloin, 12 to 20 ounces, trimmed of fat
3 cups apple juice
¼ cup maple syrup

I tablespoon oil
4 apples, peeled and diced
½ cup dried cherries
2 rosemary sprigs
I pinch hot pepper flakes
¼ cup sugar
¼ cup apple cider vinegar
3 pounds potatoes, boiled and drained

3 tablespoons roasted garlic
¼ cup Romano cheese
¼ cup Gorgonzola cheese
¼ pound butter (I stick)
½ cup heavy cream
2 tablespoons sour cream

Salt and pepper, to taste
½ bunch asparagus
I tablespoon olive oil
I teaspoon chopped garlic
I pinch dried oregano
I pinch dried basil

Marinate the pork tenderloin in the apple juice and maple syrup for 2 hours. Grill to desired doneness.

In a sauté pan, heat the oil. Add the apples, and cook until just tender. Add the dried cherries, rosemary, hot pepper flakes, sugar and vinegar. Cook until the sauce thickens and coats the apples and cherries.

In a large mixing bowl, combine the potatoes, roasted garlic, cheeses, butter, heavy cream and sour cream. Whip until smooth. Season to taste with salt and pepper.

Marinate the asparagus in the oil, garlic and dried herbs for at least 30 minutes. Drain and grill until tender. Serve the grilled pork tenderloin with the apple-cherry sauce, mashed potatoes, and asparagus.

Recommended wine: *Artesa Carneros Chardonnay*

Sharing their culinary secrets...

Chef Nino D'Urso, Capriccio

Chef Tony Morales, Café Fresco

Chef Nick Rabar, Chow Fun Food Group
(XO Steakhouse, Ten Prime Steak & Sushi,
Big Fish, Citron Wine Bar & Bistro)

Chef Tim Kelly, Café Nuovo

Chef Gene Allsworth, Table 28

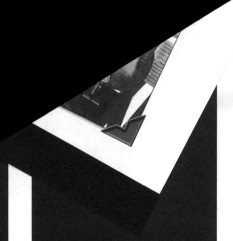

Hearty, flavorful and delicious.

Chefs: Salvatore Cefaliello
and Louis Forti

Owner: Alan Costantino

Cuisine: Italian

Specialty: Fresh pasta dishes

Signature dish: Ravioli like
Mama used to make

Price range: Appetizers,
$7 to $8

Entrees,
$7 to $13

Hours: Open seven days a week

Monday through Saturday,
8:30 am to 6 pm

Sunday,
8:30 am to 4 pm

BOLOGNESE SAUCE FOR PASTA

(Makes 4 cups)

¼ cup olive oil
¼ cup butter
¼ cup diced salt pork
1 large onion, peeled and diced
½ pound Italian sweet sausage meat, casings removed
½ pound lean beef, ground
4 chicken livers, chopped fine
2 garlic cloves, minced
½ teaspoon rosemary
1 bay leaf
¼ teaspoon freshly ground black pepper
¼ cup dry white wine
1 cup canned peeled plum tomatoes
2 medium-size ripe tomatoes, finely chopped
Pinch of freshly grated nutmeg
1 cup boiling water

In a large saucepan over medium-high heat, combine the olive oil, butter and salt pork. Add onions and brown slowly. Cut the sausage meat into ½-inch pieces, and add to the saucepan. Add the ground beef and chopped chicken livers. Brown slowly for 15 minutes.

Add the garlic and rosemary to the sauce along with the bay leaf and black pepper. Stir well and cook for 10 minutes. Add the wine; stir, cover and cook for 10 minutes. Using the back of a large slotted spoon, mash all chunks in the sauce until fine. Add the tomatoes and nutmeg. Remove and discard the bay leaf. Add the boiling water and cook, uncovered, for 45 minutes at a simmer. Use this sauce with your favorite cooked pasta.

Chef's note: At Waterplace, this is served with a crisp fruit and avocado "hash" and cucumber granita. The key here is the "poaching" which results in tender, succulent fish. For an extra added touch of color, drizzle each dish with 1 teaspoon of Olivado avocado oil.

Recommended wine: *Frescobaldi Brunello di Montalcino*

Just some of the friendly faces you'll meet at Venda.

Of course, made even better when it's ladled on Venda's homemade pasta.

VENDA RAVIOLI
PASTA FRESCA

Chef: Matthew P. Thomsen

Owner: Larry Lovejoy

Cuisine: Contemporary American

Specialty: Seasonal cuisine

Signature dish: Grilled Beef
Tenderloin with Crispy
Onion, Baby Carrots
and Blue Cheese Fondue

Price range: Appetizers,
$8 to $14

Entrees,
$14 to $30

Hours: Open seven days a week

Lunch on
Monday through Friday
from 11:30 am to 2:30 pm

Dinner on
Monday through Saturday
from 5 pm to closing

Dinner on Sunday
from 4 to 8 pm

*There's not a heckuva lot to say here except,
"Pour the wine and make me another of those, please."*

SPICY LOBSTER SUMMER ROLL

(4 servings)

½ cup pickled ginger, chopped fine, divided
1 cup tamari soy sauce
1 teaspoon sambal chili paste
1 tablespoon rice wine vinegar
1 lobster, 1 and ½ pounds, cooked and cooled
2 shallots, chopped fine
4 rice paper rounds, soaked in cold water
1 large carrot, cut into 3-inch long strips
1 English cucumber, cut into 3-inch long strips
1 daikon radish, cut into strips
1 red bell pepper, cut into strips
4 scallions
4 large shiso leaves
4 large basil leaves
8 large mint leaves

To make the sauce: In a bowl, combine ¼ cup of the pickled ginger, tamari, sambal and vinegar. Whisk to mix well. Chill before serving.

Remove the meat from the cooked lobster, and chop into very small pieces. In a bowl, combine the lobster meat with the remaining pickled ginger and shallots.

Lay out the rice paper rounds on a clean work surface. Divide the vegetable strips and herbs evenly over each round. Top with equal amounts of the lobster meat mixture. Roll up the rounds as if you were making egg rolls. Slice the rolls in half and serve immediately with the sauce.

Chef's note: Shiso leaves, which are similar to basil and mint, are available in Asian markets.

Recommended wine: *Antinori Bolgheri Vermentino*

I love recipes that meld ingredients that you would never expect to go together like mango and ancho chilis for example. That's why there are chefs! You'll love these crab cakes.

WATERMAN GRILLE

4 Richmond Square
Providence, RI
401-521-9229
www.watermangrille.com

Chef:	Michael Conetta
Owner:	Newport Harbor Group
Cuisine:	New American
Specialty:	Waterfront dining
Signature dish:	Lobster Mac'n Cheese
Price range:	Appetizers, $4.50 to $10.95
	Entrees, $12.95 to $29.95
Hours:	Open seven days a week for dinner starting at 5 pm
	Sunday brunch, 10:30 am to 3:30 pm

CRAB CAKES WITH LEMON ANCHO AIOLI

(8 servings)

Oil, as needed for frying
1 tablespoon diced red pepper
2 tablespoons diced red onion
4 cloves fresh garlic, finely chopped
¼ cup diced mango
½ cup sour cream
1 tablespoon Dijon mustard
1 pound rock crab (frozen claw and cavity meat or fresh lump crab meat)
3 tablespoons lemon Juice
2 scallions, thinly sliced on the bias
¼ teaspoon cayenne pepper
Kosher salt, to taste
Cracked white pepper, to taste
2 egg whites
1 to 2 cups panko breadcrumbs

Lemon Ancho Aioli:
1 to 2 egg yolks (depending on size)
1 tablespoon chopped fresh garlic
5 tablespoons lemon juice, divided
1 quart blended oil
Kosher salt, to taste
2 dried ancho chiles
1 tablespoon white balsamic vinegar
1 teaspoon ancho powder
½ shallot, minced
¼ cup chives, thinly cut on the bias
5 roasted garlic cloves

In a sauté pan, heat a little oil to cook the peppers, onions and garlic. Let cool. Then add the mango to mixture.

In a separate bowl, combine the sour cream and Dijon mustard. Gently squeeze the crab meat to remove excess water. Fold the crab meat into the wet mixture. Add the cooked peppers, onions, garlic and mango. Add the lemon juice, scallions, cayenne pepper, salt and pepper.

In another bowl, whisk the egg whites until fluffy and tripled in volume. Fold the eggs into wet mixture. Slowly add the breadcrumbs until you are just able to form a nice cake. They should be fragile to handle but hold together. In a hot frying pan, add enough oil to coat the bottom of the pan. Over medium to high heat, pan-sear the crab cakes on both sides. This can be done in batches, and the crab cakes can finish cooking in a 350-degree oven. The crab cakes should be crunchy on the outside and creamy on the inside.

Combine the egg yolks, garlic and 2 tablespoons of lemon juice in a food processor. Whip with the blade until the mixture visibly thickens a little. Slowly add the oil until the aioli becomes thick in texture like mayonnaise. Taste to see if it's "yolky" in flavor. If it is, add a little more oil until the flavor fades. Season with salt. Once you have this base, you can add flavor. Reconstitute the anchos in warm water. Deseed and skin, if needed. Puree the anchos with the white balsamic vinegar. Combine the ancho puree, ancho powder, minced shallot, chives, roasted garlic and remaining lemon juice. Add to the aioli. Once the aioli is incorporated, taste it. Adjust with seasoning if needed.

Recommended wine: *Cloudy Bay Sauvignon Blanc*

WATERPLACE

1 Finance Way
Providence, RI
401-272-1040
pinellimarrarestaurants.com

Very fresh, clean and healthy, perfect for the spring and summer months

OLIVADO POACHED CHILEAN SEA BASS
(4 servings)

4 (6-ounce portions) fresh Chilean sea bass
1 bottle Olivado avocado oil
Kosher salt and black pepper, to taste

Season the sea bass with salt and pepper. Place the sea bass in a medium-size sauté pan.
Pour the oil over the fish until it is totally covered.

Place the pan on medium-low heat until the oil reaches a temperature of about 180 degrees
(use a thermometer to determine this). Once that temperature is reached, continue cooking for
5 to 7 minutes, or until the fish is light and flaky and no longer opaque. Using a spatula, remove
the fish from the pan. Before serving, carefully drain on paper towels to absorb excess oil.

Chef's note: For an extra added touch of color, drizzle each dish with 1 teaspoon of Olivado
avocado oil.

Recommended wine: *Nobile Icon Sauvignon Blanc*

Chef: Angie Armenise

Owners: Bill Pinelli and
Steve Marra

Cuisine: Contemporary/Infusion

Specialty: Pork and seafood

Signature dish: Sea Bass

Price range: Appetizers,
$7 to $11

Entrees,
$12 to $28

Hours: Tuesday through Sunday,
11:30 am to closing

Steve and Bill

Chef Angie

WEST DECK

1 Waites Wharf
Newport, RI
401-847-3610
www.thewestdeck.com

Chef: Robert Biela

Owners: Michael Cheney and
Kevin Stacom

Cuisine: Eclectic

Specialty: Seafood and steak

Signature dish: Filet Mignon
with Stilton Cheese Butter
and Port Wine Demi Glace

Price range: Appetizers,
$7.50 to $13.50

Entrees,
$21 to $33

Hours: Open seven days a week
in the summer.

In the winter,
open Thursday through Sunday,
5:30 to 11 pm.

Also offers Sunday brunch.
Call for hours.

A fresh, creative approach to calamari.
A delicious alternative. The currants and almonds make it.

SAUTÉED CALAMARI IN BROWN BUTTER
WITH BLACK CURRANTS, ALMONDS AND SPICY HUMMUS

(4 servings)

1 and ½ pounds calamari rings, fresh or frozen
2 tablespoons Chinese five-spice powder
½ cup toasted almond slivers
½ cup dried black currants

Spicy Hummus:
    2 cups cooked chickpeas
    1 tablespoon sambal chili sauce
    2 tablespoons tahini paste
    2 tablespoons olive oil
    2 tablespoons water
    Salt and white pepper, to taste
    ¼ cup unsalted butter
    Pita bread, for serving

Toss the calamari in the five-spice powder. Set aside for 5 to 10 minutes. Toast the almonds in a 350-degree oven until golden brown. Allow to cool. Combine the almonds with the currants. Set aside.

In a food processor, combine the chickpeas, chili sauce, tahini paste, oil, water, salt and pepper. Process until smooth. Set aside.

In a large sauté pan over high heat, melt the butter until it turns brown, then add the calamari. In the same pan, add the almonds and currants. Sauté for 30 to 50 seconds, only until the calamari is firm but not overcooked. On a large serving plate, place the hummus in the center. Pour the calamari on top. Garnish with pita bread, which can be toasted or grilled. Serve immediately.

Recommended wine: *Schiopetto Pinot Bianco*

TV Maitre d' Diary... Made this for dinner guests. Blew them away!
Oh man, the macadamia nut butter is addictive!

FILET MIGNON WITH MACADAMIA NUT BUTTER

(4 servings)

2 (8-ounce) bunches of asparagus
Olive oil, as needed
4 large scallops
¼ cup macadamia nuts
½ pound unsalted butter, at room temperature
¼ cup truffle oil
1 bunch chives, half minced and half whole (for garnish)
Salt and pepper, to taste
4 (10-ounce) filet mignon steaks
Canola oil, as needed

Preheat grill and preheat oven to 450 degrees.

Rinse and trim the ends of the asparagus, then cut each stalk into thirds. Place the asparagus on a baking sheet. Drizzle with olive oil. Season with salt and pepper.

Slice each scallop thinly to get pieces that resemble quarters. Make each slice as thin as the next. You should end up with about 8 slices per scallop. Shingle the scallop slices in a circle with no middle hole, and tuck the last slice under the first. You should end up with 1 round of scallops for each steak.

In a food processor, grind the macadamia nuts. Add the butter, truffle oil, minced chives, salt and pepper. Season the steaks with olive oil, salt and pepper. Grill the steaks for 10 minutes on each side to achieve medium rare (15 minutes for medium). Rotate the steaks occasionally. When the steaks have 5 minutes left to cook, place the asparagus in the 450-degree oven, and roast until done but still firm.

Place a skillet or nonstick pan on high heat. Add a little canola oil to the pan. Season the scallops with salt and pepper. Place the scallops in the pan. When the bottom edges of the scallop rounds begin to brown, turn off the heat. Do not flip the scallop rounds.

To serve, arrange 8 to 10 roasted asparagus pieces in the middle of each dinner plate in a haystack formation. Place the steaks on each mound. Top with 1 tablespoon of the macadamia nut butter. With a spatula, carefully invert each scallop round and place on top of each steak so that the seared side of the scallop round faces up. The heat from the steak will finish cooking the scallop rounds from the bottom for a perfect medium rare scallop. Garnish with a few long chives. Serve immediately.

Recommended wine: *Moniz Vineyards Syrah Spring Mountain*

ZOOMA BAR-RISTORANTE

245 Atwells Avenue
Providence, RI
401-383-2002
www.zoomari.net

Chef: Jeff Burgess

Owners: Dr. James Cardi and
                Joseph F. DeQuattro

Cuisine: Southern Italian

Signature dish: Sauté di Calamari

Price range: Appetizers,
                        $7 to $15

                        Entrees,
                        $15 to $30

Hours: Open seven days a week

            Sunday through Thursday,
            11:30 am to 1 am

            Friday and Saturday,
            11:30 am to 2 am

Zooma Chef Jeff Burgess studied with renowned Chef Mario Batali in Italy and also worked at Batali's restaurant Babbo in New York City. Let me tell you, he learned a thing or two about calamari! "Hey, ma-ma, zooma, zooma, baccala!"

SAUTÉ DI CALAMARI
(1 serving)

6 tablespoons corn or vegetable oil
1 cup all-purpose flour
2 tablespoons cornstarch
6 ounces calamari
2 garlic cloves, roasted
6 cherry tomatoes, cut in half
2 large pinches kosher salt
¼ cup white balsamic vinegar
Parsley, as needed for garnish

In a 12-inch sauté pan, add the oil and heat to 350 to 375 degrees. Sift the flour and cornstarch together. Coat the calamari with the flour mixture. Shake off any excess flour. Add the calamari to the sauté pan. Fry until golden brown on one side. Using tongs, carefully flip the calamari over and fry the other side for 30 seconds. Add the roasted garlic and tomatoes. Carefully drain the oil from the pan. Season the calamari with salt. Toss to coat well. Deglaze the pan with the vinegar. Pour all the contents from the pan onto a large platter, garnished with parsley, if desired.

Recommended wine: *Riff Pinot Grigio*

RECIPE INDEX

SANDWICHES

MAIN DISHES
Beef

Chicken/Duck/Ostrich

Lamb

Pork

Fish/Seafood

Joe Zito *is the host, writer and executive producer of* **TV Maitre d'**, *southern New England's top-rated television restaurant showcase, a regular fixture for many years on Fox Providence and WPRI-12. Joe combines a 30-year media presence on radio, television and in print as a humorist, commentator and feature writer, with more than 25 years of proven restaurant experience as a waiter, captain, general manager and, of course, maitre d', from Rhode Island to Beverly Hills, California. His proven ability to speak the language of restaurateurs and chefs has made his television show a breakout hit for everyone from the restaurant insider to the casual diner. Recognized as engaging and glib, Joe is right at home behind the "mic," in front of the camera, and now in your kitchen. A native Rhode Islander, Joe resides in East Greenwich with his wife Nancy, his son Mark, and his 18-inch plastic statue of Dean Martin.*

Linda Beaulieu *is the author of three books: Divine Providence: An Insider's Guide to the City's Best Restaurants, The Grapevine Guide to Rhode Island's Best Restaurants, and The Providence and Rhode Island Cookbook. Winner of the prestigious James Beard Award for magazine writing, Linda has been published in numerous local and national publications. She is a graduate of Northeastern University, Boston, where she majored in journalism. Linda now owns and operates Beyond Words, a small public relations firm that specializes in restaurants and chefs. She is a producer of Costantino's Roundtable, a local PBS television show that explores the food and wine scene in Rhode Island. A native Rhode Islander, Linda and her husband Brian live in Lincoln with their cocker spaniel, Beau, and they have a summer home with a much-used outdoor kitchen in Narragansett.*

THE TV MAITRE D' COOKBOOK

Your Guide to the Best Restaurants in Southern New England

Featuring Their Secret Recipes

The TV Maitre d' Cookbook features recipes from more than 100 of the finest restaurants in Rhode Island and nearby Massachusetts and Connecticut. It also offers current information on those restaurants concerning location, phone numbers and hours. This book is perfect for people who like to cook as well as people who love to dine out. It's the perfect gift for local residents, families who have just moved to the area, tourists, people on business trips, clients, customers, friends and relatives.

This popular book can be purchased by filling out the form below and mailing it with a check for $25 payable to **The TV Maitre d' Cookbook**. This includes tax, shipping and handling costs.

Send your order form and check to: **The TV Maitre d' Cookbook**
1615 South Road
East Greenwich, RI 02818

This cookbook and restaurant guide can also be purchased in bulk at a discount. The minimum wholesale order is 10 copies. If you are interested in a bulk purchase, please call Joe Zito at 401-595-3399 or Linda Beaulieu at 401-728-6688.

Thank you for your order.

Name _____

Address _____

City/Town State Zip _____

Would you like your book autographed? ☐ YES   ☐ NO